# Day of Defense

## Positive Talking Points for the Latter Days

# DAY OF DEFENSE

## Positive Talking Points for the Latter Days

SCOTT THORMAEHLEN

CFI PUBLISHING
AN IMPRINT OF CEDAR FORT, INC.
SPRINGVILLE, UT

ISBN 13: 978-1-4621-1172-5

Published by CFI, an imprint of Cedar Fort, Inc.
2373 W. 700 S., Springville, UT 84663
Distributed by Cedar Fort, Inc., www.cedarfort.com

LIBRARY OF CONGRESS CATALOGING-IN-PUBLICATION DATA

Thormaehlen, Scott, 1982- author.
Day of defense : positive talking points for the latter days / Scott Thormaehlen.
pages cm
Includes bibliographical references and index.
Summary: Addresses red flags and stigmas that people have with The Church of Jesus Christ of Latter-day Saints, and explains that Mormon doctrines are based on Biblical teachings and the original church that Christ established.
ISBN 978-1-4621-1172-5 (alk. paper)
1. Church of Jesus Christ of Latter-day Saints--Doctrines. 2. Mormon Church--Doctrines. I. Title.

BX8635.3.T46 2013
289.3'32--dc23

2013002146

Cover design by Rebecca J. Greenwood
Cover design © 2013 by Lyle Mortimer
Edited and typeset by Michelle Stoll

Printed in the United States of America

10 9 8 7 6 5 4 3 2 1

"WE ARE NOT DIVIDED,
ALL ONE BODY WE,
ONE IN HOPE AND DOCTRINE,
ONE IN CHARITY."

—*"Onward Christian Soldiers"*

# Contents


Acknowledgments.......................................................................... xi

Introduction............................................................................... xiii

1. From a Single Faith to Many: *Judaism, Christianity, and Islam*..... 1
2. The Great Apostasy: *No More Prophets or Apostles?*.....................11
3. What Is a Christian?: *Post–New Testament Traditions*................. 23
4. More than One Wife?: *Plural Marriage*....................................... 39
5. Man's Relationship to God: *Premortality and Man's Potential*......47
6. The Afterlife and Salvation: *One Heaven and One Hell, or Three Degrees of Glory?*.......................................................... 63
7. Salvation: *Saved by Works or Grace?*............................................73
8. More than One Book?: *The Book of Mormon*..............................81
9. Many Reforms, One Restoration: *Joseph Smith and the Primitive Church*...............................................................91
10. Other Misunderstandings: *Answered with the Bible*...................101
11. Be One: *The Great Gathering*...................................................115

Appendices.....127

Appendix I: *Adam, the God Pattern, and World Religions*.....129

Appendix II: *The Old Testament as the Starting Point to Find the God Pattern*.....133

Appendix III: *Biblical Law and Superstition*.....135

Appendix IV: *Helpful References and Graphics*.....137

Bibliography.....141

Index.....147

About the Author.....153

# Acknowledgments

I would like to acknowledge my family and friends who in one way or another helped me to develop this analysis of my faith and many of life's questions in general. Specifically, I would like to thank two trailblazers—my grandmother Linda Waldron McKissick and my mother, Jeri McKissick Thormaehlen—for being positive influences and examples of the restored gospel and for choosing to move from Idaho and making their home in Texas. To my father, E.J. Thormaehlen Jr., for his example of what it means to hold the priesthood in the LDS faith. To my mentor and family friend, the late Dr. Jim Cowart, MD, for assisting me in the early edits of this book and providing scriptural insight. To another family friend and MD, Dr. Joe Cannon, the stake president from my home stake—thanks for the positive influence he has had on my family.

Finally, I want to think the staff at Cedar Fort, Inc., for helping me sharpen and focus some of my discussion, particularly Jennifer Fielding for representing my book as my first acquisitions editor and her replacement, Catherine Christiansen, for her patience and input. To the designer, Rebecca Greenwood, who captured the message of the book with a simple but crisp cover design. To my editor, Michelle Stoll, for making the final edits and suggestions.

I hope you enjoy the content of this book and regard it as a necessary addition to your personal library of religious literature.

# Introduction

In 2011 and 2012, the media had a conversation about what the world knows as "Mormonism." This conversation was very one-sided, and, according to the esteemed PEW Research Center, "America's 'Mormon moment' is over, and public opinion appears to be little changed. Eight-in-ten Americans (82%) say they learned little or nothing about the Mormon religion during the presidential campaign" (Pew, *Americans Learned Little About the Mormon Faith, But Some Attitudes Have Softened*). That is not an option for Latter-day Saints. The Restoration of Christianity is not a "moment," nor is it "over."

In 2012, the Salt Lake City, Utah–based *Deseret News* reported:

> From time to time, Mormons are thrust into the public spotlight. . . . Yet the permanent things that ground their inner lives in this changing religious landscape are often left out of the picture. The Mormon understanding . . . rarely finds a place in the public narrative. That bigger picture is essential to understanding who Mormons are. (Walker, "Looking for understanding in the Mormon spotlight")

Walker quotes Dr. Jan Shipps, a non-Mormon scholar of LDS history and theology, who said: "Mormonism is a really complex theological system. All of its parts fit together beautifully. But if you just know a little bit about one of them, or part of them, it seems weird" (ibid.).

Few in the world truly understand Mormon beliefs—perhaps because there are only fourteen million members scattered across the earth, or maybe because the "Mormon Church," as it is known today, has only been around since AD 1830. In short, the LDS Church's primary claim has always been that it exists because the original Christian church, though flourishing, was on its way toward division and apostasy, which the apostles began to witness (see chapter 2).

The primary goal of *Day of Defense* is to act as a guide to help Mormons and those interested in Mormonism be aware of common misconceptions and negative commentary that create a wall between the world and the truth of the Restoration. In an article published during the 2012 election season by the *Salt Lake Tribune*, Peggy Stack—editor of *Dialogue: A Journal on Mormon Thought*—made the statement that "Mormons don't have a terribly sophisticated rubric for dealing with negative commentary, either from within or without the church" (Stack, "Are Mormons Primed for Persecution in this Election Season?" *Salt Lake Tribune*). This book was written to help initiate within the LDS community a "sophisticated rubric" for dealing with the misconceptions and accusations surrounding Mormon beliefs.

According to the Church's public relations representative, Michael R. Otterson, "The five most common stereotypes of members of the LDS Church [are] that they are not Christian, that they belong to a cult, that they are insular and secretive, that they are weird, and that they practice polygamy" (Walker, *Journalists urged to allow Mormons to define themselves*).

My hope is that the reader will come away from reading this book with a clearer way to talk with others about these kinds of issues. *Day of Defense* addresses the common misconception that Mormons are not Christian because Mormons do not accept post–New Testament traditions such as the doctrine of the Holy Trinity, "one heaven and one hell," infant baptism, the Bible as the only source of God's word, the definition of a saint, and other characteristics that have been embraced by much of the Christian community over the centuries.

Considering all the work that so many reformers and religious thinkers have accomplished throughout Christian history, to stop at their conclusions and pretend nothing more can be discovered leaves many out of the conversation and only perpetuates misunderstandings and divisions. *Day of Defense* will rely heavily on the Bible to bring into light several misunderstood LDS beliefs.

As perfect as truth is, when it is amid humans in written form, it allows for a variety of opinions. It must be admitted that God, the author of order, is organized, and while men freely interpret God's word in their own ways—for good or for bad—many institutions have been created out of One God.

Since the formation of The Church of Jesus Christ of Latter-day Saints, the world has not given the "Mormons" much respect. The most popular motive for persecuting Mormons came because of polygamy. Other reasons included disbelief in Joseph Smith's claim he found golden plates and had visions. However, the Bible is full of angelic visitations and stories of plural marriage, and some archaeological findings show that ancient writing on metal plates is not a ridiculous concept after all. If the critics then and especially today could understand that arguments over such issues are ill-founded, Mormons would probably be more understood, and there would be no need for this book.

Joining the conversation about religion will open our minds to who we are, where we have been, and where we are going as a society, a nation, and a world, as well as where we're headed in the hereafter. Pondering religious questions should not be left only to theologians and church authorities. If only "authorities" could ask these questions, how would an individual define their personal relationship with the Almighty? Wisdom is a gift for all of God's children to obtain. When a proclaimed religious leader speaks to us, it is wise to take his or her words to the written word and then to personal prayer, searching for confirmation of truth or error.

Each chapter begins by briefly stating the negative commentary that critics bring against Mormonism, then goes on to illustrate where and how Mormon theology fits with the Bible and in the overall historical context.

This book seeks to show that the Bible covers Mormonism and to help mend the way much of the world perceives Mormonism in relation to Christianity and the ancient text. Seeking common ground should build bridges between people of every denomination. Significant to these aims is the acknowledgement of a pattern—the "God-pattern," or what could also be termed the "single-faith system of the Bible." I define this "God-pattern" as "one faith patterned throughout the entire Old Testament, fulfilled by Christ and his Apostles, but which fell away to await a final dispensation." The central characteristics of each biblical dispensation included the continuation of scripture and a prophet (or prophets) called by God. This faith system or pattern is also characterized by several biblical concepts discussed in each successive chapter, built upon the premise that God, in this day, has prophets on the earth as he did throughout the Bible's history.

Renowned Christian author C. S. Lewis wrote, "People need to be reminded more often than they need to be instructed. The real job of every moral teacher is to keep on bringing us back, time after time, to the old simple principles" (Lewis, *Mere Christianity,* 82). By examining several misconceptions about Mormonism, this book provides evidence that Mormon beliefs, or Joseph Smith's "new inventions," have a biblical foundation, that Smith is "bringing us back . . . to the old simple principles." The burden of proof to say otherwise rests with the critics of Mormonism.

**Chapter 1** begins with a brief overview of Western faiths—Judaism, Christianity, and Islam—showing a shared origin in the Old Testament of the Hebrew text and the nature of their differences. Keeping these ancient religious splits in mind throughout the rest of the book provides much-needed context to answer why there are so many religious traditions, what happened to the single-faith system, and how the Bible shows that God always called prophets to distinguish false belief from true religion.

**Chapter 2** gives a history of early Christianity, including the time during and shortly after the life of Christ's Apostles. The loss of leadership after the Apostles died resulted in what is known to Mormons and other Protestant groups as the Great Apostasy. Apostasy is a common theme throughout the Old Testament, and it happened to the New Testament Church as well. Then, in God's appointed time, he called a prophet to restore his single-faith system to man once again.

**Chapter 3** will describe how the faith that Christ established spread far and wide amid the dominant Greek and Roman cultures. The influence of these cultures, coupled with Constantine's need to tighten his grip over the Roman Empire, led to heresy through the mixture and adoption of Greek and Christian ideas.

This combination transformed Christianity into an institution far removed from the New Testament church. Post–New Testament traditions will be compared to the Bible text and approached from the LDS perspective.

**Chapter 4** tackles the most well-known misconception about Mormons—polygamy, or plural marriage. This doctrine is explained in light of the Bible and portrayed as both a legitimate marriage practice and a gross perversion if practiced without the consent of a prophet. This chapter will illustrate that the Bible and other LDS scripture complement one another and there are specific parameters clearly defined for this misunderstood practice.

**Chapter 5** puts to rest the argument that Mormons are polytheistic in the traditional sense and explains the doctrine that men and women have divine potential to become gods and goddesses in the next life, as described in the scriptures. The focus of this chapter discusses a pre-earth existence and the nature of God, again in light of the Bible and evidence from other early Christian writers.

**Chapter 6** continues to shed light on how Mormons differ from what over the centuries has become mainstream Christian thought. This chapter compares the idea of "one heaven and one hell" with the three degrees of glory revealed to Joseph Smith. This chapter also talks about the afterlife and degrees of glory in the resurrection, as described in the New Testament and in writings from other early Christian writers.

**Chapter 7** discusses the long-debated subject that pits Protestants, Evangelicals, and nondenominational churches against Catholics in regards to salvation: Do our works save us, or are we saved by grace alone? Mormons are usually categorized (along with the Catholics) as believing they have to "earn their way to heaven." Biblical religion is often viewed as having a God who relished in punishing those who did not serve him. Latter-day Saints believe God asks his followers to *do* certain things. LDS critics confuse these "works to save us" or to "earn our way to heaven" with what is simply abiding by the teachings of Christ and his Apostles. Modern revelation and current Church policies are practiced based on New Testament teachings that some may argue are vague, such as baptism for the dead. In the end, the LDS faithful are taught to cultivate Christian character and principles into their lives.

**Chapter 8** gives a summary of the Book of Mormon: what it is, its context in relation to the Bible, and idiosyncrasies people encounter as they read the book.

**Chapter 9** talks about the Restoration of the primitive Christian Church again to the earth in 1830 through Joseph Smith Jr. This chapter explains beliefs that Mormons share with mainstream Christianity, mainstream beliefs that Mormonism rejects, and biblical beliefs that are unique to Mormonism—supporting the claim that not only are Mormons Christian, but they are Christian in the truest sense of the word.

**Chapter 10** covers some miscellaneous issues unique to Mormonism and explains the LDS perspectives on alcohol, worship services, missionaries, temples, and more.

**Chapter 11** wraps up by examining Christ's teachings to individuals: to free themselves from addiction, to serve one another, and to be engaged in building the kingdom of God. This chapter discusses Christian unity, also including Muslims and Jew who share a common origin.

Speaking on defending one's faith, Scott Lloyd, a writer with the *Church News*, reported on an annual conference for the Foundation for Apologetic Information and Research, or FAIR. At this conference, Daniel C. Peterson, a professor of Islamic studies at BYU and an LDS apologist, described the purpose of apologetics. Lloyd reported that "Apologetics, in the sense of defending one's beliefs, is actually an older derivative from the Greek term apologia than are words that connote expressing regret or sorrow." At the conference, Peterson cited 1 Peter 3:15, Paul's admonition to "be ready always to give an answer to every man that asketh you a reason of the hope that is in you with meekness and fear." Peterson described that the word "answer" in this passage "is the Greek word apologia, or apology." What it means to "defend" one's faith, then, is not to apologize, but to simply explain one's belief. "Socrates, Origen of Alexandria, Thomas Aquinas, John Locke, and C. S. Lewis are among historical figures he mentioned who belong to the 'venerable' tradition of apologetics" (*Church News,* Lloyd).

At the October 2007 general conference, Elder M. Russell Ballard said, "The growing prominence of the Church and the increasing inquiries from others present us with great opportunities to build bridges . . . and pass on accurate information. But it can also present a greater possibility of misunderstanding . . . if we allow others to define who we are and what we believe rather than presenting it ourselves" (Ballard, *Faith, Family, Facts, and Fruits*). The primary aim of this book is to provide positive commentary with which Latter-day Saints can compassionately and confidently talk to their friends and family about the Restoration and what the world knows as Mormonism.

*"Behold, how good and how pleasant it is for brethren to dwell together in unity!"*

—Psalm 133:1

*"One Lord, one faith, one baptism."*

—Ephesians 4:5

1

# From a Single Faith to Many

## Judaism, Christianity, and Islam

### Red Flags and Misconceptions:

*God is too big for one religion.*

The Old Testament provides insight to the belief in one God and one faith. It confidently states that, among many false gods, the God of Abraham, Isaac, and Jacob represents that there was always one true religion in the face of many. One does not have to be Mormon to understand this truth laid out plainly in the Bible. This chapter isn't meant to disparage other faith systems, but rather to provide a historical context for the existence of the Mormon faith and to ask what happened to the singular faith led by prophets of God.

In contrast to the singular God of Western belief systems, new-age philosophy proposes that there are many paths of spirituality, discounting the idea of one Savior or one God. New age has a distinct background from these biblical religions. Jews, Muslims, and Christians are confidently grounded in their belief in the God of Abraham, Isaac, and Jacob as the God of all. With no dogmas, formal leadership, or ancient scripture, new age religion lacks historical basis for their gods or spirituality, while the Bible speaks of all people having at one time or another some connection to the families, tribes, and nations spoken of in its history (Slick, CARM). But what gives rise to the popularity of new age religion and the rejection of the God of Israel? How does one reconcile the divisive results that the ancient Hebrew faith has created in these three mainstream traditions?

Let's review how Judaism, Christianity, and Islam—which all believe in the God of Abraham, Isaac, and Jacob—diverged from one another. My point here is not to condense these entire belief-systems into a few paragraphs, or to speak on their behalf, but rather to touch on their key distinctions and disagreements. In reexamining the common origin of these three faiths and where they diverged into their modern forms, we investigate which of the three is the continuation of the single-faith system in the Bible. The basis for the single-faith system is admittedly biased in that Christ and his apostles continued or carried the Old Testament torch forward to the Gentile nations. Muslims and Jews will not agree with this premise, but the purpose of this book is to look at Christianity at large from a Mormon's perspective.

While Judaism, Christianity, and Islam possess the same origin in the Holy Bible, particularly in the Old Testament, their primary disagreement arises in the specifics and nature of Jesus Christ's divinity. Their theological disagreements have, sadly, served only to deepen the hatred and violence toward each other. Each religion is discussed in more depth below.

With this question before us—that is, which of these three faith-traditions parallel or continue what is laid out in the Bible?—I believe Mormonism with its Restoration doctrines can bridge the differences among these religions and shed light on biblical truth. Such questioning and conclusions are meant to provide a historical backdrop for showing that Joseph Smith, with heaven's help, established what Christian reformers hoped for: a restoration of primitive Christianity (for Christians), and a return to the God of Abraham, Isaac, and Jacob (for Jews and Muslims).

## Islam

The origin of Islam began six centuries after Christ and his apostles preached and walked the earth. Muhammad, born in the

### Timeout: Man's "Religion" Problem

Instead of using the term "religion" to describe a system of worship, I believe God's "single-faith system" sounds much more real and relates more exactly to the faith of those in the Old Testament, New Testament, Book of Mormon, and modern times. (In other words, "one Lord, one faith, and one baptism.") I'm hoping to expose a pattern that has existed in previous times to remedy man's "religion" problem: that of the divisions/counterfeits of true religion that have been used for personal gain, government dominance, and anything corrupt that "religion" is often associated with in history. Since religion is receiving a negative treatment more and more every day by secular, progressive, and agnostic groups, I hope to show the LDS faith in a positive light, that it fits into the biblical pattern, and that it is organized the way God organized his gospel throughout the scriptures.

Arabian city of Mecca, was a well-traveled man who came into contact with and was influenced by the religious squabbling between Christians and Jews. Muhammad sought the truth and prayed often, eventually claiming to be called of Allah (God) by the angel Gabriel; his mission was to restore the lost Abrahamic faith (since Jews and Christians believed in the same God but possessed no answers to heal doctrinal differences).

The Muslims regard the "lost faith" Muhammad restored as the continuance of the biblical line of prophets from Abraham, Moses, and Jesus. Their holy text, the Qur'an, states:

> Say (O Muslims): We believe in Allah and that which is revealed unto us and that which was revealed unto Abraham, and Ishmael, and Isaac, and Jacob, and the tribes, and that which Moses and Jesus received, and that which the prophets received from their Lord. We make no distinction between any of them, and unto Him we have surrendered. (Surah Al-Barqarah 2:136)

The Qur'an states that Muslim origin lies in "The Book"—the Old Testament—and that Muslims revere Christ as a prophet. Islam rejects Christianity because Jesus said he was the Son of God and because, like Judaism, Islam is a monotheistic faith, a belief in only one god.

For Islam to remain consistent with itself after 1,400 years, a few questions must be asked. First, where is the prophet of Allah denouncing radical activity today? Islam answers by saying that Muhammad is believed to be the last in the line of prophets. After so many centuries, has God spoken again? If so, to whom? About what? Why has he spoken again after so long? And what would the result look like if God spoke to man in more recent times? In the last decade Islam has come to the forefront in the media because of the violence and terrorism from a few of its most radical members. Surely while Islam seeks to be understood by the world as a peaceful faith, in its most desperate hour they could use another prophet to proclaim truth, peace, and righteousness.

Second, Islam eventually divided into a variety of groups arguing over differing translations of the Qu'ran and the means by which Islamic leaders were chosen after the death of Muhammad. The groups became known as Sunni, Shia, Sufi, and radical extremists. Which branch is correct? Or are they all wrong? By what standard are we to determine which branch is more consistent with "The Book"? In comparison, Christianity too has divided with different sects, losing its unity and falling into apostasy (explained in chapters 2 and 3). Perhaps like Christianity, without the leadership of their prophets and apostles, Islam too experienced their own apostasy?

Lastly, the Bible is key because the Qur'an mentions, reveres, and borrows from it. So rather than analyze Islam as a whole and how much good or evil can come from this belief system, why not ask some of these questions and inquire where modern Islam fits in with the biblical text that preceded Muhammad? Though practices have evolved differently in their respective cultures over the centuries, the shared belief of Mormonism and Islam in the Old Testament provides the starting point toward better dialogue between people of both faiths. After exploring various Mormon restored doctrines in this book, perhaps historians, scholars, researchers, and member of the LDS faith may be able to further create an honest dialogue.

### Judaism

The tribe of Judah, or the Jews, remain a covenant people; however, they are without a prophet and a continuation of scripture. Mormons and Christians differ from Jews in that they believe

Jesus is the Savior of mankind while the Jews still await the Messiah's arrival. Anciently, as a result of their disobedience to God and constant attraction toward idolatry, the Israelites were carried off and enslaved by the Babylonians and Assyrians for a number of years. Five hundred years before Christ, Israelites were allowed by the Persian King Cyrus to return to their homeland, where the Jews began to reestablish their faith. Unfortunately, their faith relied solely upon the written word and man's interpretation without the authority and continual direction of prophets.

The earliest roots of *modern* Judaism are found in the Jewish sect of the Pharisees, a new Jewish tradition that formed after their release from captivity. The Pharisees, like the Sadducees who also sought to get back to their pre-captivity faith, were a religion without a new prophet, founded upon their own interpretation of the scriptures. Today Jews consider the Hebrew Bible and other rabbinical teachings (Jewish writings and oral teachings before the time of Christ) to be inspired. Since captivity, no other prophets have been called in the Jewish religion, nor has God directed them to rebuild the temple. The last prophet of the Jews was Ezra of the Old Testament, some five hundred years before Christ. From the Christian perspective, Christ and his apostles filled this void of leadership and continued the consistency of the Old Testament with a much stronger representative among them—that of God being in flesh among men. In reality, Christianity actually began with a strictly Israelite membership, which shows that Christians and Jews have more in common than the labels we modernly accept and apply to ourselves to distinguish one group from another.

A major stumbling block between the Jewish and Christian religions rests on some fifty prophecies in the Old Testament about Jesus Christ's life, mission, crucifixion, and role as the Savior for all mankind. The Jews' rejection of Jesus as their Messiah is where Jewish and Christian traditions diverge from one another. Christians view Christ as the God of the Old Testament with the same administrative authority to bestow upon his apostles, the same authority given to Moses and Aaron, for example. Like Muslims, Jews also believe that God has not continued to call prophets. Both traditions have since fallen from the biblical use of prophets.

## Christianity

Just as Islam and Judaism have seen many reforms and contradictions since their origin, so has Christianity. Christianity has divided into so many divisions that it has become difficult to define true Christianity. This dilemma seems to add fuel to the fire of irreligion, atheism, and alternative spiritual lifestyles.

Most of the modern Christian divisions formed after Martin Luther and the Protestant Reformation. However, before these divisions, even early Christianity experienced the division that the apostles strongly warned against; some groups maintained their ancient Hebrew roots, others influenced by the Greek and Roman cultures were Hellenized, and others became the Gnostics, who focused on knowledge and reason. As the early church became divided and gospel principles became lost or muddled in local cultures, Constantine took advantage of this situation at the Council of Nicaea. He gathered bishops from across the empire, who then counseled and debated, formed the beginnings of their formal doctrine and church, and persecuted those who resisted. Division, pride, and the death of the apostles morphed the loving missionary church that Christ established into a state-run political belief system that violently considered everyone else heretics. This state-sanctioned faith system eventually became the Catholic Church.

The reason for Christian division in modern times comes from men seeking to return Christianity to its roots. Some do so by emphasizing particular doctrines (for example, the gift of tongues or, for a more extreme example, the snake handlers of the Eastern United States Appalachian denominations) or by delegitimizing others to make their brand appeal to their audiences. However, without a prophet from God, the religious free-market furthered division, interpretation, and denominations.

Today, Latter-day Saints are privileged to have living apostles and prophets, who provide the spoken word (words spoken by prophets), a significant characteristic of the biblical single-faith system. (Recall that at each time in the Bible, whether with Abraham, Moses, or Jeremiah, these men represented the spoken word, and they also had the written word, which could be added to by later prophets.) Find a time in this single-faith system when God had a people and a prophet but added no new scripture. It's not there!

Modern LDS apostles and prophets speak with authority equal to the scriptures, or the written word. Today's spoken word (which further adds to the LDS written word when printed) provides clearer interpretations to the ancient written word, much like Jesus did during his time on earth. The written word of his time was, of course, the Old Testament. Throughout the Gospels, Jesus provided further revelation and corrected the doctrines that the Pharisees and Sadducees formulated after the Babylonian captivity. Just as Joseph Smith restored truth and added what appears to be new and unfamiliar information to mainstream Christian doctrines, Jesus too taught things contrary to men's interpretation of the scriptures in his time. He also revealed newer mysteries not known to previous generations (see Colossians 1:26) in a rather bold ministry that led to his martyrdom.

I believe the source of division exists simply because of different interpretations of the Bible. The Bible, as a volume of ancient manuscripts written by prophets in their own time, is a witness that God and the true faith have been with man since time began. The idea of one true faith appears cyclical in the Bible, in which Israel's neighboring nations are portrayed as blatantly wrong idol-worshippers with no apologies. The Bible leaves no other possible approach for man to seek the divine: it does not allow for one-God-several-faiths, many-gods-many-faiths, or no-gods-no-faith. In the Bible, there was always one.

### Why One May Be Confused about Mormons

Critics of Mormonism, who can be found in various Christian denominations and elsewhere, produce "anti-Mormon" writings, books, and websites and set aside time during their church services to discuss wrong religions and cults. Often, the target of mainstream Christianity's religious bigotry is aimed at Latter-day Saints. A good example of LDS criticism came from a news article in reference to the 2008 United States presidential candidate Mitt Romney. Though Romney received support from the prominent Bible college Bob Jones University in South Carolina, the university described Mormons in this way, exposing their lack of understanding:

> The influential Christian college . . . teaches . . . [that the] Mormon

> church is a cult. . . . Evangelicals may not agree with the tenets of [Romney's] Mormon faith or even the standing of The Church of Jesus Christ of Latter-day Saints as a Christian faith. . . . Non-Christian theologies . . . [are] completely opposed to the doctrines of Mormonism." (*Mitt Romney finds Christian Support,* AP)

If Bob Jones University, by assigning the term "cult" to Mormonism, means to call the LDS Church "a system of religious rites and observances zealously devoted to a person" (Funk and Wagnall's Dictionary), then admittedly the name on the buildings Mormons use for religious rites and observances clearly states, "The Church of JESUS CHRIST of Latter-day Saints." Mormons are, in word and deed, zealously loyal to Christ and his faith system.

Why would people label a church titled "The Church of *Jesus Christ* of Latter-day Saints" as unchristian? Some acknowledge Mormons' belief in Christ; others do not or, more extremely, say Mormons preach a "different Jesus." As critics distribute anti-Mormon literature, they create a lot of these packaged attacks that float around unchallenged. At the beginning of each chapter, negative commentary aimed at the LDS faith will provide the reader with a context of how "Mormons" are discredited by people who read the same Old and New Testament. These persistent misconceptions do not serve well for an enlightening dialogue toward Christian unity and, further, unity between biblical faiths.

The Bible says the truth will set you free. Such truths are not reserved solely for scholars or clergy. Out of respect to members of all religions and acknowledging that our differences remain unsettled, asking the tough questions and allowing history and their texts to speak for themselves have led to the conclusions found in this chapter and the source of religious divisions. The remainder of this book leaves the broader debate between the three Western faiths in this chapter and turns the focus toward the debate Mormons have with their critics, who are often fellow Bible believers.

## Conclusion

> "The essence of Mormon doctrine is that God has revealed to us specific answers . . . about the purpose of earth life. We do not claim to have all the answers, but we rejoice in those which we

have. . . . Because we have been given these answers in a very special way, we wish to share them with others. We do not do this out of any sense of smugness or superiority, but because we sincerely believe that what we have to offer the world will contribute to the well-being and happiness of our fellow humans, both in this life and the next." (Johnson, *Jews and Mormons*, 188)

Below are a few core commonalities Mormons share with Jews, Muslims, and other Christians:

1) They all have ties back to a pattern that relied on God calling new prophets and continuous scripture.
2) Mormonism, like Islam and Judaism, seeks a restoration of the Abrahamic faith.
3) Mormonism, like some Christian denominations, seeks to restore early Christianity.

In light of the negative commentary at the heading of this chapter and the deep divisions that have spawned from the God of Israel, it seems hopeless that any inspired source of truth exists that can unite man and stay the hand of societal ills that are often brought on by immoral action, disobedience to the laws of God, and human pride. All three of the major faith branches have fallen out of step with the Bible, having no prophet. However, if the source of healing lies in the calling of prophets and contemporary revelation, as is God's pattern, then The Church of Jesus Christ of Latter-day Saints has something to offer in its claim of being a restoration of primitive Christianity with additional scripture and living prophets and apostles.

*"[The Church is] built upon the foundation of the apostles and prophets, Jesus Christ himself being the chief corner stone."*

—Ephesians 2:20

*"And it was given unto [the Devil] to make war with the saints, and to overcome them: and power was given him over all kindreds, and tongues, and nations."*

—Revelation 13:7

# 2
# The Great Apostasy
## No More Prophets or Apostles?

### Red Flags and Misconceptions:

*God is too strong for his church to fail—no apostasy.*
*There are no more prophets.*
*The office of "Apostle" was limited to the original twelve.*

The previous chapter showed that both Islam and Judaism are faith systems that go on without a modern prophet. This chapter places most of Christianity in the same category, as another major religion that no longer has revelation through prophets. In contrast to these three major faith-systems, Mormons do believe in modern revelation. The ninth LDS Article of Faith states, "We believe all that God has revealed, all that He does now reveal, and we believe that He will yet reveal many great and important things pertaining to the Kingdom of God." And as the proverb says, "Where there is no vision, the people perish" (Proverbs 29:18).

The spoken word is needed to properly interpret the written word, and prophets have served as God's spiritual mouthpiece for both. While the scriptures, or the written word, have never ceased to exist among man, the lack of continuity in the spoken word has allowed man to interpret the written word at his free will, thus creating these three major religions. Latter-day Saints believe the restoration of the spoken word has come through modern prophets and apostles, as well as through revelation given to Joseph Smith Jr.

Does the New Testament end the practice of calling prophets, as mainstream Christians believe, leaving us with the scriptures as the final authority coupled with commentary from local ministers or preachers? Was the office of Apostle only limited to the original twelve? Critics of Mormonism would have you believe the answer to both questions is *yes*. But at what point did God cease to be the same today, yesterday, and forever?

The teachings found in the New Testament express certain principles and show the type of organization, officers, and ordinances (such as baptism, marriage, and healing the sick) that are characteristic of the New Testament church. Over time, logic insists that without clear leadership, the written words and organization are likely to become unclear, mistranslated, absorbed, or simply lost to whatever cultural or political influences are the strongest. In the case of the New Testament church as it moved west, the dominant cultures of the Greeks and Romans proved too much for a church without apostles.

Whenever God wanted his word spoken, he revealed it through a prophet, who then recorded it. That is the consistent pattern. Without prophets (including the Mormon belief in modern revelation) comes confusion and division! Among the three religions (Judaism, Islam, and Christianity), those who today do not rely on prophetic guidance remain divided. Mormons believe that apostasies are associated with times of confusion, a loss of spiritual gifts, and divisions. Specifically, Mormons believe the death of the original Twelve Apostles led to the great apostasy.

### Apostasy and Restoration: A Repetitive Pattern

While God is omnipotent, he is bound to the covenants he makes with his children, and the pattern of apostasy and restoration is seen throughout the Old and New Testaments. God's power is not diminished, but the power of the covenants is in direct relation to man's righteousness. In Doctrine and Covenants 82:10 it says, "I, the

Lord, am bound when ye do what I say; but when ye do not what I say, ye have no promise." The argument that God is too powerful for his church to fail goes directly against biblical evidence of this pattern of apostasy and restoration. A detailed chronological illustration of such a cycle can be as follows: Before an apostasy can occur, there first has to be an established covenant with a prophet and people. Second, the established covenant ends with the withdrawal of the Spirit (apostasy) due to rebellious hearts, pride, and persecution of the prophets. The Lord speaks of this withdrawal in Genesis 6:3, which says, "My spirit shall not always strive with man."

This pattern began with Adam, the first prophet, when he disobeyed God, was thrown out of the garden, and was restored to God's grace again in mortality. The pattern repeated with Noah, who lived in a time where only eight people survived their apostasy. The earth was flooded, the wicked were removed from the earth, and the Lord restored another righteous generation through the prophet Noah. Again, after generations of wickedness and the apostasy that culminated in the Tower of Babel, God found grace in Abraham, which led to another restoration, or covenant. Generations following Abraham, Joseph the son of Jacob (Israel) was sold into Egypt. The Israelites were eventually taken into bondage by the Egyptians. After fleeing Egypt, their constant yearning for the false gods they had left behind is a clear example that the generations of Israel between the prophet Joseph and Moses were in an apostate condition.

Through an experience with the divine, another prophet, Moses, records the words found in the first five books of the Bible, commonly known as the Five Books of Moses. Moses again restores Israel to the truth with the Exodus and the Ten Commandments. Time and time again throughout the rest of the Old Testament, Israel falls into false idol worship, and many times prophets such as Isaiah and Jeremiah call the people to repentance. After Israel is taken into bondage to Babylon and later released, two sects of mainstream Jewish belief emerge—the Pharisees and the Sadducees—whom Jesus corrected on many occasions and sought to return to the faith that he restored, preached, and fulfilled.

Adam, Noah, Abraham, Moses, later Old Testament prophets like Isaiah and Jeremiah, Jesus and his apostles, and Joseph Smith all had something in common: their time on earth was associated with an apostasy, a restoration, or both. This pattern shows that God is bound by his covenants with mankind. If men are unfaithful, apostasy follows. However, when men follow God's word, they are blessed with divine leadership through prophets and revelation.

### An Old Testament Reference to a Post–New Testament Apostasy: "Famine of the Word"

Toward the end of the Old Testament, the prophet Amos speaks of a gap in prophetic inspiration in what he called a "famine of the word." Amos 8:11–12 describes a famine in the land, not of bread or water but of the hearing of the words of the Lord. Those seeking the word would search for it and not find it, we are told.

An apostasy occurred between the Old Testament and the New Testament, but it was not the apostasy Amos referred to. It was an apostasy in the sense that they lacked the higher priesthood without prophets, authority, and revelation. Luke chapter 1 provides evidence that the prophecy of Amos had not yet been fulfilled. Zacharias, the father of John the Baptist, was a priest who practiced in the temple of the Lord. It can be concluded that Zacharias and other Jews who were clearly living in the period preceding the birth of Christ had in their possession the words of the Old Testament. There are several examples in which Christ alludes to the Jews not understanding the scriptures. In order for them to be misunderstood, they must have access to the words. Jesus said, "Ye do err, not knowing the scriptures, nor the power of God" (Matthew 22:29). The Gospel of Matthew also states that Christ "taught them as one having authority, and not as the scribes" (Matthew 7:29). When the Pharisees come to tempt Jesus (Matthew 19:4), Jesus asks, "Have ye not read?" While the Pharisees had the word, they lacked a prophet with authority to provide interpretation and further revelation.

Recall that Amos prophesied there would, at some future time, be a famine of the word, wherein people would seek and not be able to find. As evident from the examples above, throughout the New Testament there was access to the scriptures (Old Testament), so the Jews were able to *find the words*.

The famine Amos spoke of began as the New Testament closed and was completed with the martyrdom of the apostles. Later, as laymen had less access to the words because of illiteracy and the lack of printing, they relied on their priests to teach them, often in a foreign tongue. The Protestant Reformation highlighted the end of this apostasy and is proof that such a famine occurred as Amos declared nearly two millennia before.

## New Testament Warnings: Division and Change

### Acts 20:29–31

In verse 31, there is one key statement by Paul: "that by the space of three years I ceased not to warn every one night and day with tears." This is very powerful because Paul had tirelessly warned the saints of impending danger and division, and this after he had just said in verse 29 that "After my departing shall grievous wolves enter in among you, not sparing the flock." *Not sparing the flock?* Those sound like strong words for one to believe that the church did not experience an apostasy shortly after Paul's ministry.

### 1 Corinthians 1:10

In this verse, the Apostle Paul further exhorts the saints, "that there be no divisions among you; but that ye be perfectly joined together." He goes on in verse 11 to say, "There are contentions among you."

### Galatians 1:6–8

Paul says, "I marvel that ye are so soon removed from him that called you into the grace of Christ unto another gospel. . . . But though we, or an angel from heaven, preach any other gospel unto you than that which we have preached unto you, let him be accursed."

Critics of the LDS faith use this scripture to lead one to think Joseph Smith's vision fulfills Paul's warning, but does it? To begin with, Paul's warning is specifically to the Galatians. Furthermore, Joseph Smith's claim that Christianity fell into apostasy is described in verse 7 of this chapter, that some were already working to pervert the gospel. This fact, coupled with the eventual death and extinction of the office of apostles, conveys the potential for some, or all, to pervert the gospel as these scriptures warned.

With such a loss to early Christianity, how would the truth be restored in the future? Verse 8 says "though we, or an angel from heaven." I understand verse 8 as Paul describing the pattern of authority, coupling the apostles with the angel as the only two sources of authority: 1) an apostle called by Christ and 2) revelation from heaven. In fact, verse 9 warns of a false gospel *from man*. What was the Council of Nicaea? It was a gathering of men separated by generations from the apostolic authority, and this council resulted in much of how mainstream Christians still view doctrine. Finally, if there is any concern over what verse 8 actually means, Joseph Smith saw God and his son; the warning to the Galatians was to beware of *man* perverting the Gospel.

### 2 Timothy 1:15

Paul states to Timothy "that all they which are in Asia be turned away from me." According to historian J. G. Davies, Asia Minor "continued to be the Christian country, *par excellence*" (Davies, *The Early Christian Church*, 86). Davies verified that this area was significant in early Christian conversions and population compared to most other areas beyond the second century. If Paul witnessed fallen Christians in Asia Minor, what do Davies's findings mean? That the people of Asia Minor continued in their religion without apostolic authority and worshipping in their own brand of Christianity? How else can Paul's words be taken, other than that the divisions he feared—in 1 Corinthians 1:10 for example—have become reality? The apostles warned against division, and they clearly witnessed it during their ministry.

### 2 Timothy 4:3–4

"For the time will come when they will not endure sound doctrine; but after their own lusts shall they heap to themselves teachers, having itching ears; and they shall turn away their ears from the truth, and shall be turned unto fables." Paul's prophecies about the decline of the early Church in this example continue to show the trend that the prophet Amos predicted centuries before the apostles.

### 2 Peter 2:1–2

Peter also warns the saints that "there shall be false teachers among you, who privily shall bring in damnable heresies, even denying the Lord that bought them, and bring upon themselves swift destruction. And many shall follow their pernicious ways; by reason of whom the way of truth shall be evil spoken of."

REVELATION 13:7

John sees in his vision a beast, representing evil, which was allowed to "make war with the saints, and to overcome them: and power was given him over all kindreds, and tongues, and nations." This vision further describes imminent apostasy and persecution of those who believe in Christ. Discussed later in the next chapter are different interpretations of what a "saint" is, and that makes a big difference as to who this verse is prophesying about.

Both the Old and New Testament clearly predict the imminent doom of the early church through a changing of doctrine and an eventual lack of access to the word. These are warnings to the New Testament Christians, the very Christians of the first century. These Christians reflect those who Mormons believe died with the priesthood authority and whom Mormons profess to be a modern reflection of—not the fourth-century Christians (whom Catholics reflect) or the seventeenth-century Christians (which "mainstream Christianity" is based on). These verses, in their descriptions of what the apostles witnessed, clearly show the early church in danger, much like ancient Israel is time and time again throughout the Old Testament.

## Biblical Delegation of Priesthood Authority

A common theme throughout the Bible is the calling of prophets—delegating the priesthood authority of God to a man—with the eventual loss and restoration of that power. Today, if a faith is to claim it represents the Bible, performs ordinances such as baptism and the laying on of hands, and ordains individuals to church offices such as bishops and deacons, it must do so in a manner compliant with the Bible. God's pattern of delegating the priesthood powers to his prophets contrasts man's giving authority to man through academic training or theological degrees. Aside from Mormonism, only Catholicism relies on apostolic succession, while all other forms of Christianity rely on seminary or theological training to be ordained into the ministry. What does the Bible say about receiving such authority? The Bible offers such an answer in both the Old and New Testaments.

First, in Exodus 28:1, God says to Moses (his prophet), "Take thou unto thee Aaron thy brother, and his sons with him, from among the children of Israel, that he may minister unto me in the priest's office." Here God instructs his prophet to then appoint those of God's choosing for offices in the church. Likewise, Hebrews 5:4 recognizes the authority of Moses, a prophet of God, saying ,"And no man taketh this honour unto himself, but he that is called of God, *as was* Aaron" (italics added).

Second, the prophet Samuel receivs direct contact with the Lord in 1 Samuel 3. In verse 1, it describes Samuel's period of the Old Testament as one in which "there was no open vision," meaning there were no prophets on the earth. This chapter continues with the story of Samuel's call to God's work. In verse 20 it says that "Samuel was established to be a prophet of the Lord." Samuel received God's authority to act directly in his name and to lead the Israelites.

Third, Paul does not become an apostle simply from his vision on the road to Damascus. In his apparition on the road to Damascus, the Lord instructs Paul to go to Ananias in Damascus to be baptized (see Acts 9). It is quite clear that Paul has to pass through the proper channel of authority, just as Aaron received his authority from Moses.

Paul, who appointed Titus, states in Titus 1:5, "For this cause left I thee in Crete, that thou shouldst set in order the things that are wanting, and ordain elders in every city, as I had *appointed* thee" (emphasis added).

A man must receive the proper power and authority by the laying on of hands given personally by Christ, his apostles, or those designated by his apostles, such as Titus was. An early example of the laying on of hands is recorded in Deuteronomy 34:9, where Moses laid his hands upon Joshua. A modern-day example of receiving such authority happened in the late 1820s when Joseph Smith and Oliver Cowdery received the Aaronic Priesthood from John the Baptist through the laying on of hands (Doctrine and Covenants 13). They later received the Melchizedek Priesthood in the same manner from Peter, James, and John, who were the last apostles on earth to possess these priesthood keys and who came in the latter days to restore them (Doctrine and Covenants 27).

Christ and his apostles represented the last living establishment of God's church recorded in the Bible, and several Old and New Testament scriptures point toward the fall or loss of the word once again. However, not only the word would be lost, but in following God's pattern, the priesthood authority would also be lost. In the Old Testament, the prophet Amos describes a future period as a "famine of the word." In the New Testament, Christ's apostles also warn of an imminent threat to the Church they were establishing, thus prophesying of the Great Apostasy when priesthood authority would no longer remain on the earth.

### The Twelve Apostles and Authority

One result of division and change referenced by the New Testament writers has led to the belief among mainstream Christians that there were only twelve men called as "apostles" whom Christ ordained for a specific mission only in New Testament times. LDS author Barry R. Bickmore describes the office of apostles in his *Restoring the Ancient Church: Joseph Smith and Early Christianity.* He says:

> Although Catholics since the second century have been fond of calling their church 'Apostolic,' by virtue of having descended from the churches established by the Apostles, we shall see that living Apostles are meant to be part of the true Church of Christ, and a Church cannot be 'Apostolic' without Apostles. Some have espoused the idea that the Apostles were just twelve men whom Christ ordained for a specific mission—and thus were no longer needed. . . . However it is admitted by some prominent Christian scholars that the Apostles 'did not live to see the Church fully organized and at work,' and the New Testament is quite clear that when vacancies occurred in the Twelve they were promptly filled. (*Bickmore, Restoring the Ancient Church, 31*)

Beyond the original Twelve, several others were called to be apostles. Matthias filled the vacancy left open by Judas (Acts 1:23–26). Paul also mentions his call to be an apostle (1 Corinthians 1:1). According to Acts 14:14, Barnabas and Paul receive their call to be apostles. In Galatians 1:19, Paul says, "Other apostles saw I none, save James the Lord's brother." If God's pattern continued to call prophets and apostles when vacancies arose, the apostleship would have seen the church "fully organized and at work." We see from the New Testament examples that the original Twelve were replenished, but historically the office was lost as leadership was killed and the Great Apostasy ensued with the loss of the main line of authority through the prophets and apostles.

The death of the prophets and apostles resulted in the loss of the established pattern of delegating priesthood authority. In light of these dire conditions, at what point did God again restore his authority to Christendom to call popes, cardinals, pastors, priests, or preachers, and was it in a way that was similar to how Aaron, Samuel, or Paul were bestowed with authority?

## Conclusion

Apostasies are a common theme illustrated throughout the Bible, and two thousand years ago the church that Christ established fell away—as did the faith systems of each previous prophet. The falling away of Christ's church does not indicate a weak God; rather it harkens back to a principle taught in Genesis—that God's "spirit does not always strive with man." This is due to man's nature to often succumb to pride and worldliness, thus rejecting his covenants with God.

In conjunction with this rejection of covenants, man also rejects God's prophets and apostles, and in the process, this authority or these offices are lost to future generations until God calls another prophet. Christ has said he is "the same yesterday, and to day, and for ever" (Hebrews 13:8), and a prophet under proper authority has always led his established covenant people. Why would he deviate from his own pattern of calling a prophet to lead his church?

Finally, while others claim that the office of the original Twelve Apostles was restricted to the New Testament church, evidence concludes that vacancies were filled to maintain leadership in the Church. With the martyrdom of Christ's Apostles, this rejection brought the church of the New Testament faith-system into what Mormons describe as the Great Apostasy. However, the restoration of calling prophets and apostles in modern times continues God's pattern of calling these offices to lead his church. This pattern has been reestablished in The Church of Jesus Christ of Latter-day Saints.

Years ago, a scholarly member of the Roman Catholic Church came to visit the Mormons in Salt Lake and explained his attitude toward the two religions:

> You don't even know the strength of your own position. It is so strong that there is only one other tenable in the whole Christian world, and that is the position of the Catholic Church. The issue is between Catholicism and Mormonism. If we are right, you are wrong; if you are right, we are wrong; and that's all there is to it. The Protestants haven't a leg to stand on. For, if we are wrong, they are wrong with us, since they were a part of us and went out from us; while if we are right, they are apostates cut off long ago. If we have the apostolic succession of St. Peter, as we claim, there is no need of Joseph Smith and Mormonism; but if we have not that succession, then such a man as Joseph Smith was necessary, and Mormonism's attitude is the only consistent one. It is either the perpetuation of the gospel from ancient times, or the restoration of the gospel in latter days. (Richards, *A Marvelous Work and A Wonder*, 3)

Based on the Catholic scholar's statement, his acknowledgement of the historical ties and the structure of the LDS Church with apostolic succession show that Mormonism, if investigated in biblical context, is not as strange or mysterious as critics portray it to be.

*"For laying aside the commandment of God,*
*ye hold the tradition of men."*

—Mark 7:8

*"I hear that there be divisions among you; and I partly believe it.*
*For there must be also heresies among you."*

—1 Corinthians 11:18–19

# 3

# What Is a Christian?

## Post–New Testament Traditions

Red Flags and Misconceptions:

*Mormons don't believe in the Trinity, so they are not Christian.*
*The Bible is the only source of God's word.*
*Baptizing babies secures salvation.*
*The term "saint" is reserved for miracle-workers.*

The last chapter discussed the offices and authority of the church and the eventual extinction, once again, of prophets and apostles. With this lack of leadership, like in the previous biblical times, men continued to practice the teachings and doctrines they had learned, but they didn't have the spoken word to provide clarification. This sometimes resulted in the creation of new traditions and well-intentioned customs but often led to divisions and the creation of multiple sects. Christ experienced difficulty in his time teaching the Pharisees and Sadducees because they were so entrenched in traditions, rites, and their own interpretation of the Old Testament. Another example of wrestling with the traditions of men or the errors of their ways is found in Abraham fleeing from his fathers to seek the one true God (Genesis 11–12 and Abraham 2:5, 13).

The Great Apostasy of the early Christian church eventually led to new traditions that evolved over the centuries and eventually divided into multiple Christian sects. The confusion and subsequent division that ensued with the death of the Apostles came from the lack of authority and continual revelation, which encouraged Constantine to gather the remaining local authorities (bishops) to the Council of Nicaea. This council ushered in the creation of what would become the Roman Catholic Church. As this new entity sought to create its identity and unity, traditions not originally espoused with or evidently written in the text of the New Testament became associated with what it meant to be a Christian. Among these interpretations and traditions, Mormons view the following as some of the post–New Testament traditions that were adopted: the Holy Trinity, the Bible as the only source of God's word, infant baptism, and the worship of saints, to name a few. Because Mormons do not espouse these doctrines, many people do not consider them to be Christians.

This chapter questions doctrines Christianity has adopted that seem to deviate from the first-century church, post–New Testament traditions without clear New Testament support. But what is a Christian? Must a Christian accept doctrines that were not part of the teachings of Christ?

Speaking in terms of the fourth-century creed that defines the Holy Trinity, LDS Apostle Jeffrey R. Holland says the following in an article entitled "Are Mormons Christian?": "Arguing that Mormons are not Christians because they do not recite the Nicene Creed would leave Jesus and his disciples outside the Christian fold as well" (Burke, *Are Mormons Christian?*).

### Post–New Testament Doctrines Enter In

The post–New Testament creeds and doctrines that mainstream Christians still accept and that were adopted so long after the life of Christ illustrate the underlying problem and evidence that man moved Christianity toward traditions beyond the New Testament. That Joseph Smith's revelations sought only to reverse that trend—to go back to the New Testament—speaks volumes to his divine calling.

Below is a list of Catholic practices that evolved over the past two millennia. This partial list comes from an article printed in *Foundation Magazine* by M. H. Reynolds, entitled "The Truth About Roman Catholicism":

- Peter as the first "pope" and the existence of "popes" versus prophets in early Christianity
- Prayers for the dead (AD 300)
- Doctrine of purgatory (Gregory I, AD 593)
- Prayers to Mary and dead saints (AD 600)
- Worship of the cross (AD 786)
- Celibacy of the priesthood (AD 1079)
- Indulgences (AD 1190)

Such a list illustrates well-intentioned doctrines or ideas that entered in centuries after the faith system of Christ and his Apostles. It is not to say these practices are evil, but it has to make one wonder where the foundations for such practices are found in the doctrine of the New Testament. More importantly, by what measure does accepting or rejecting these doctrines define a "Christian"?

In the list above of post–New Testament traditions, celibacy of priests contrasts with Matthew 8:14, which describes Peter as a married man. While Catholics believe Peter was the first pope, they do not acknowledge the fact that he had a wife. Instead, they focus more on Paul's letter to the Corinthians (1 Corinthians 7:1–7), which they interpret as a requirement for their church leadership to practice celibacy. A closer examination of this letter from Paul suggests that fornication (see verse 2) leads men to burn (verse 9). Paul, as a widower, is encouraging the unmarried and widows to avoid immorality outside the bonds of marriage (verse 8). He also states for those who "cannot contain" that "it is better to marry than burn" (verse 9). The New Testament mentions that bishops and deacons are to be the husband of one wife. For men dedicated to serving the Catholic Church to not receive holy matrimony is entirely inconsistent with thousands of years of biblical history where God's leaders were married. Paul's challenge to remain chaste is consistent with God's commandment "Be not deceived: neither fornicators, nor idolaters, nor adulterers . . . nor abusers of themselves with mankind . . . shall inherit the kingdom of God" (1 Corinthians 6:9-10).

Further, the practice of indulgences—a payment to the church in order to absolve one from temporal punishment that often favored those who could afford to pay—perverted Christ's teachings of repentance and substituted them instead with a means of financing the church. In Acts 8:20, Peter said, "Thy money perish with thee, because thou hast thought that the gift of God may be purchased with money." Martin Luther, a Catholic priest, targeted the practice of indulgences because it went directly against the New Testament teachings. With the advent of the printing press and exposure to God's word in their native languages, Europeans all over, like Luther, began exploring different ideas. This began the Protestant Reformation, which intended to restore Christianity back to its biblical roots.

## Popes versus Prophets

How are prophets and popes different? They both claim to hold the priesthood of God and hold the keys to lead God's people. However, prophets follow God's pattern of being ordained through direct communication with God whereas Popes are elected at the Papal Conclave, where cardinals select the new Bishop of Rome. Admittedly, popes fill a role similar to "bishops," or local authorities during New Testament times. History remains unclear as to the exact point at which the offices of bishop, popes, and cardinals replaced apostles. Catholics vehemently claim that this particular organization and process stemmed from the New Testament apostolic authority. However, without an authorized, written text from one of Christ's apostles describing this transition—and after centuries of papal changes in doctrines—we cannot be sure that this change in organization truly originated in Christ's church. Mormons understand that their beliefs are restored first-century Christian beliefs.

Are popes infallible, as Catholicism declares? Perhaps the differences between the actions of a biblical prophet and the popes in the post–New Testament era are distinguished by two significant "Christian" events that occurred during the Dark Ages and were endorsed by the popes: the Christian Crusades and the Inquisitions. Islam, Christianity, and Judaism were at the center of the conflict during the Crusades. The Crusades were Christian wars meant to reclaim the Holy Land—Jerusalem—from Muslim invaders. The land was home to the Jews and various sacred sites that hold meaning to the three major religions. During the Crusades, popes offered forgiveness for sins and salvation for those who fought. These wars and papal forgiveness were unnecessary for salvation since Christ is the only way to the Father. Biblical prophets are not recorded acknowledging any other means of salvation but through God, their Redeemer, and his commandments.

The idea behind the Spanish Inquisition calls into question whether the popes acted in the name of God or not. In Spain during the 1400s, King Ferdinand wanted a stronger hold over his people. He believed that by wiping out all the Jews and Muslims, he could have a completely Catholic country, and therefore better control. The Inquisitions "were similar to other institutions of government and discipline in early modern Europe. The earliest, largest, and best-known of these was the Spanish Inquisition, established by Pope Sixtus IV at the petition of Ferdinand and Isabella, the rulers of Aragon and Castile, in a papal bull of Nov. 1, 1478" (Britannica, *facts about Sixtus IV and Spanish Inquisition*). The argument could be made that everything Christ and his apostles stood for is tarnished in the eyes of some truth-seekers for these very actions done in Christ's name, thousands of years after his ministry. Contrary to the violent and intolerant actions exhibited during the Inquisition and the Crusades, Christ preached, "Blessed are the peacemakers" (Matthew 5:9).

## Restricted Access to the Word

In John 5:39, Christ exhorts, "Search the scriptures; for in them ye think ye have eternal life: and they are they which testify of me." During the Middles Ages, religious sanctions limited the common man's access to Christ's teachings at a time when the printed word was becoming more available with the advent of the Gutenberg printing press. The papal authority believed that if widespread publication of the Bible reached every common man, each would develop his own ideas, which would have disrupted the ability of church authorities to maintain unity in doctrine. Further, it also posed a threat to the political and economic control of the church.

In the sixteenth-century Council of Trent, the Oxford Constitutions in 1408, and other church edicts issued during the Middles Ages, access of the word was restricted to the lay members by outlawing publication of the scriptures without permission from Catholic church authorities. Other examples of keeping the word from the lay members included banning the distribution of Bibles and preaching to parishioners in Latin rather than in their native tongues. Several significant figures who inspired the Protestant Reformation and more liberal access to the scriptures for all and who were martyred for their supposed heresies include John Wycliffe, William Tyndale, and Sir Thomas More (Wilcox, 49). Christ exhorted his followers to read and understand the scriptures. The Great Apostasy and the loss of priesthood authority led to a dark time in which this became nearly impossible because of the risk of excommunication or even death.

## Doctrine of the Holy Trinity

One of the favorite issues that critics of Mormonism use to separate Mormons from the Christian fold is that Mormons do not accept the doctrine of the Holy Trinity, but rather believe in what the Bible calls the Godhead (Acts 17:29, Romans 1:20).

The LDS belief in the Godhead consists of the Father, Son, and Holy Spirit. All are God, but unlike the doctrine defined in the Nicene Creed, they are not one personage; rather, they are three separate beings, perfectly united in will. The mainstream Christian idea of the Holy Trinity is that of three persons in one entity, something beyond which man is meant to fully understand.

What does the Bible say about Christ and the Father? In the chart below (Table 3.1, next page) are a number of references that illustrate the nature of God the Father and Jesus Christ. Mormons differ from the Christain majority in their belief that there are two beings, whereas mainstream Christians view God as one being who manifests himself in different roles.

In several of the references, Christ distinguishes himself by saying things—such as "I go unto my Father" and "I am not yet ascended to my Father"—that clearly delineate their distinct personages. On one hand, Mormons identify with the mainstream Christian view that the scriptures often speak of "one God." But on the other hand, Christ says, "I seek not mine own will, but the will of the Father which hath sent me" (John 5:30). Further, Ephesians 3:9 describes their oneness and Christ's own divine nature as a God—as the one whom God the Father used to create all things.

Another thing to consider is that when Christ speaks of the

**Table 3.1**
**The Father and Jesus Christ as two separate beings**

| | |
|---|---|
| Matthew 3 | Jesus being baptized, Father in Heaven, Spirit as a dove. |
| John 3:16–17 | He gave his only begotten Son, . . .God sent His Son. |
| John 14 | In My Father's house. . . .<br>I go unto my father. . . .<br>I go unto the Father<br>. . . for my Father is greater than I. |
| John 20:17 | I am not yet ascended to my Father . . . and your Father, and to my God, and your God. |
| The Acts 7:55–56 | Stephen sees, in visions, Jesus standing on the right hand of God (the Father). |
| Ephesians 1:2–3 | From God our Father, *and* from the Lord Jesus Christ |
| Ephesians 3:9 | Who created all things *by* Jesus Christ |
| Ephesians 3:14–15 | I bow my knees unto the *Father of our Lord* . . . whom the whole *family in heaven* is named. |
| Hebrews 1:2–3 | God . . . hath . . . spoken unto us *by* his Son, whom he hath *appointed heir* . . . , *by whom* also he made the worlds. |

Second Coming (see Matthew 24:36 and Acts 1:7), he clearly showes his "distinctness" from the Father: he says, "But of that day and hour knoweth no man, no, not the angels of heaven, but my Father only." Can God know of the Second Coming, yet *not* know of the Second Coming? Also, in the Garden of Gethsemane and on the cross, why would Jesus pray to himself? He must have been praying to a distinct being. Describing the Father and Son as two beings challenges the long-held idea or monotheistic nature of Christianity. For more on the issue of plurality of gods and monotheism, refer to chapter 5.

Latter-day Saints believe in the Godhead, which consists of three separate and distinct beings that are Gods, unified in purpose—the Father, the Son, and the Holy Spirit. The Prophet Joseph Smith stated: "I have always declared God to be a distinct personage, Jesus Christ a separate and distinct personage from God the Father, and that the Holy Ghost was a distinct personage and a Spirit: and these three constitute three distinct personages and three Gods" (*Teachings of the Prophet Joseph Smith*, 370). Rather than teaching that they all are "one" God, LDS theology emphasizes that they are united in their objective "to bring to pass the immortality and eternal life of man" (Moses 1:39). The Father is the Almighty and Christ and the Holy Ghost come after him in power and glory. Together they make up the Godhead.

Post–New Testament history shows the Church in confusion without apostles, struggling to understand the question of God's oneness. The answer to this question became known as the Holy Trinity. To resolve the people's concerns over this seemingly difficult question, Emperor Constantine gathered together religious leadership to come to a consensus. In her book *Christ the King—Lord of History*, Anne W. Carroll said:

> The poor and uneducated . . . felt close to God because his Son was man like them. But, if Jesus was not the true god, then God could seem distant and unapproachable. Intellectuals preferred a distant God; the ordinary people wanted a God they could see, hear, and touch. . . . The Church of course, had always taught that Jesus was both God and Man, but the precise way in which this could be possible had not yet been worked out. . . . Dispute came to the Emperor Constantine. . . . The Emperor was worried the controversy would destroy the hard-won unity of his empire. He commanded the Bishops of the Church to meet in Council in Nicaea in Turkey, in 325. The debate thundered through the meeting hall, with the arguments finally settling on one phrase (in Greek—only one word, *homoousion*); was Christ *one in being* with the Father? (Carroll, Christ the King, 103-104)

Carroll refers to these events as disputes and debates. If the true church had existed at the time, one would easily conclude that the issue should have been resolved pretty quickly by going to the one true source for the answer, God himself, as prophets of the Bible did to lead his church. There never would have been a question had there truly been a Peter-to-pope transition of authority, or had the office of apostle persisted beyond the death of those called personally by Christ during his ministry and those who filled the vacancies that kept the office and church structure together.

## On the Trinity: Early Christian Writers on the Father and the Son

Two factors clearly emerge from the New Testament and post–New Testament history that reflect or support Mormon theology and its origins in the early Christian church. First, in the New Testament, Christ acknowledges the united will between Father and Son, while distinguishing himself as a separate personage. Second, the doctrine of the Holy Trinity came about centuries later, without authority of prophet or apostles since none were present at the debate. Joseph Smith's First Vision of Jesus Christ standing next to the Father harkens back to the vision of the Apostle Stephen, who before he was stoned to death beheld Christ standing on the right hand of the Father (Acts 7:55–56). In addition, Christ clarifies the nature of the Father and the Son to his prophet and not through the debates of men.

Jesus can be described as a "Second God," which would seem strange to say in any other church except for the LDS church and the early Christian church. Justin Martyr (AD 100–165), an early Christian apologist, says of Christ, "a second God, second numerically but not in will" (Hatch, *The Influence of Greek Ideas and Usage Upon the Christian Church*, 268). Tertullian from Carthage (AD 155–240), another early Christian writer, speaks of the Father, the Son, and the Holy Spirit saying "that They are distinct from Each Other" and "the Father is distinct from the Son, being greater than the Son, inasmuch as He who begets is one, and He who is begotten is another; He, too, who sends is one, and He who is sent is another; and He, again, who makes is one, and He through whom the thing is made is another" (Tertullian, *Against Praxeas*, 17). Christian scholar Origen (AD 182–251) spoke of Jesus as a "second God. . . . Their unity in thought, in harmony, and in identity of will are one. They are two different entities physically" (Bickmore, 114). Novatian, once known as an antipope and later excommunicated, says, "Christ was both Angel and God. . . . The unity of the Godhead is not some mysterious metaphysical oneness, but a unity of will" (Bickmore, 115). As evidence that Joseph Smith did not just pluck crazy ideas from his imagination, these early Christian writers and the New Testament lend credence to Joseph Smith's First Vision that clarifies the nature of the Father and the Son.

## Is the Bible God's Only Source for Truth?

Another reason Mormons are sometimes not considered "Christian" is that LDS theology is not confined solely to the Bible. Does the Bible contain all God has for us? A belief common among many strict "Bible-only" believers is that the very words printed on Bibles were divinely breathed onto the paper from God's mouth. This wording—that "God breathed" onto the paper—can be found translated on some New International translations of the Bible. Where in the Bible does such a miracle take place that would lead Christians to solely rely on the written word? Because we have one book (in reality a compilation of numerous books), we need no more?

The books Christians use today are considered the "canon" of the Bible. In Christ's day they did not have a "Bible," nor did Christ, his apostles, or even the Bible testify of what the canon consists of. Surely by their best efforts, the churchmen under the direction of Constantine, through a long and complicated process, accepted what books we possess today in our Bibles while omitting other manuscripts.

However, other books are mentioned in the New Testament that are no longer in existence. There are many churches that preach the Bible only, and how they arrived at this conclusion from what is shown in the chart below causes concern.

As we can see, the Bible speaks of other books of scripture that have been lost in history, including some recorded by known prophets. The Bible does not claim to be a complete and closed compilation of God's word because it speaks of these other books; in reality, it was built upon generations of inspired prophets and teachers to record God's dealings with his children. To close the Bible or to accept a "Bible Only" doctrine would not be consistent with God's pattern of continual revelation but would instead stifle communication between God and man in the tradition of God breaking down barriers or false doctrines that crept in between dispensations. One example of God asking his children to reject their cultural traditions is the Israelites, who were asked to reject the Egyptian way of life and accept Moses, a new law, and the Ten Commandments. In addition, when Christ asked the Jews to accept his mission, as a fulfillment of the Law of Moses, traditions and cultural barriers led many to reject these teachings.

**Table 3.2**
**Lost Books of the Holy Bible**

| | |
|---|---|
| Joshua 10:13 | The book of Jasher |
| 2 Samuel 1:18<br>1 Kings 11:41 | Acts of Solomon |
| 2 Chronicles 12:15 | Shemaiah the prophet |
| 2 Chronicles 13:22 | Iddo the prophet |
| 1 Chronicles 29:29 | The book of Samuel the Seer<br>The book Nathan<br>The book of Gad |
| 2 Chronicles 9:29 | The book of Nathan the Prophet<br>The prophecy of Ahija<br>The visions of Iddo |
| 1 Corinthians 5:9 | Another epistle is mentioned |
| 2 Colossians 4:16 | An epistle to Laodicea |
| Jude 1:14 | The book of Enoch |

## Infant Baptism

Do infants require baptism to enter the Kingdom of God? Of all the differing Christian beliefs, infant baptism is a good example of an obvious post–New Testament doctrine. In mainstream Christian faith systems, infant baptism is seen as essential to salvation and overcoming Original Sin; Adam's sin caused all mankind to be guilty and therefore in need of salvation as quickly as possible, in the event that the infant dies before receiving the sacrament of baptism. In contrast to the doctrine of Original Sin, Romans 5:12–14 states that Adam's sin brought death into the world, but for people to be guilty of sin they had to have the law and transgress it. So any individual born is subject to death but not to the guilt of Adam's transgression. LDS doctrine teaches that "man will be punished for their own sins, and not for Adam's transgression" (Articles of Faith 1:2). A single Bible passage can resolve this issue: Matthew 19:14–15 speaks of infants and children as "the kingdom of Heaven," meaning they are innocent in the sight of God.

Baptism is a saving ordinance. The tradition of baptizing babies was adopted when Catholic clergy interpreted this practice to be doctrine centuries after the apostles, but there is no theological origin identified in the Bible relating to infant baptism. According to LDS Apostle Bruce R. McConkie, children "are saved through the Atonement and because they are free from sin. They come from God in purity; no sin or taint attaches to them in this life; and they return in purity to their Maker" (McConkie, *The Salvation of Little Children*, April 1977).

According to LDS theology, a merciful God requires only those who arrive at an "age of accountability" (or those who are teachable and know right from wrong) to be baptized. McConkie continues: "Accountability does not burst full-bloom upon a child at any given moment in his life. Children become accountable gradually, over a number of years. Becoming accountable is a process. . . . In our revelation the Lord says, 'They cannot sin, for power is not given unto Satan to tempt little children, until they begin to become accountable before me.' (Doctrine and Covenants 29:47)" (McConkie, *The Salvation of Little Children*).

Baptism is necessary for those who know the law and sin, requiring repentance from those sins. Revelation given to the Prophet Joseph Smith in section 68 of the Doctrine and Covenants states that at eight years old (exceptions may include mental or learning disabilities) a boy or girl is prepared to covenant with Christ, setting them on the path to learn more and progress in the Church throughout their lives. As it is recorded time and time again in the New Testament, teaching and exhorting people to repentance always preceded baptism.

Further, the Book of Mormon prophet Moroni clarifies:

> Behold I say unto you that this thing shall ye teach—repentance and baptism unto those who are accountable and capable of committing sin; yea, teach parents that they must repent and be baptized, and humble themselves as their little children, and they shall all be saved with their little children. And their little children need no repentance, neither baptism. Behold, baptism is unto repentance to the fulfilling the commandments unto the remission of sins. But little children are alive in Christ, even from the foundation of the world; if not so, God is a partial God, and

> also a changeable God, and a respecter to persons; for how many little children have died without baptism! (Moroni 8:10–12)

## Are You a Saint?

Is the term "saint" identified in the Bible as a special designation for one who performs miracles? In the traditional Catholic belief, a saint is a Christian who is held in higher regard than the rest, who has performed at least two miracles in their life, and who is thoroughly examined and approved by the papacy before being given the title of "saint." Is the foundation of this interpretation grounded in the New Testament? The term "saint(s)" is cited sixty times from Acts through Revelation, where the term "Christian" is only used three times, and the word "disciple" is used twenty-six times. Nowhere in those sixty mentions are saints described as individuals revered above other members of the congregation. Again, most of the New Testament after the Gospels opens up addressing the congregation of believers as "saints."

One example is when Paul begins with "Unto the church . . . at Corinth, to them that are sanctified in Christ Jesus, *called to be saints*, with all that in every place call upon the name of Jesus Christ our Lord" (1 Corinthians 1:2, italics added). So what is a saint? In Greek, "saint" simply means "holy." A saint simply refers to a follower of Christ: one who is sanctified, or made holy, through his blood.

So where did early Catholic clergy derive their definition of what it means to be a "saint," and why did this doctrine continue throughout the centuries into modern times? Did it persist from a longstanding, traditional belief or from the scriptures?

The Catholic reverence of saints, though well intended, seems to go beyond the mark and create a hierarchy of worship, placing "saints" just below the worship of Jesus and Mary. On the other hand, the LDS position has been to restore doctrine of the New Testament and defines a saint similar to how Paul does—a member of the church. The LDS faith has adopted this into the name of their Church, being The Church of Jesus Christ of Latter-day *Saints*.

## Conclusion

Mainstream Christianity accepts the definition or doctrine of the Holy Trinity to define the natures of God the Father, the Son, and the Holy Spirit. Catholics, Protestants, nondenominationals, and Evangelicals accept this definition without question, knowing that man debated and came to a consensus that God would be defined in this way.

Mormonism also believes in the same God of the Old Testament that all these groups worship. The central figure of the LDS Church is Christ, or Jehovah, who came to atone for the sins of man, revealed his Father, and gifted the Holy Spirit to man as a companion when Christ ascended to the Father. Mormons refer to the nature of these three separate Gods, united in purpose, as the Godhead, which is mentioned in the New Testament, but there is no mention of a "Trinity." As opposed to a debate among men, Mormonism received its answer through a prophet, and as illustrated, the evidence in this chapter supports the theology. However, critics seek to focus on fourth-century traditions that emerged as the true definition of a Christian, leaving Mormons outside the discussion when in reality the dogmas of the LDS faith reflect consistent New Testament and early-Christian doctrine. Those who seek to discredit Joseph Smith by referring to "his" religion as a cult fail to recognize the link between the Restoration and the original teachings of Christ and his Apostles.

Another dividing characteristic by which critics separate Mormons from the Christian fold is that Mormons do not accept the Bible as a closed book. The lost books of the Bible that are mentioned in Table 3.2 (papge 33) prove that the Bible was not simply handed down to us in its complete form, and nothing suggests otherwise that accepting the Bible as the only source of God's word is a defining characteristic of the Christian faith. God's pattern has always been to reveal his word to man through prophets and additional scripture.

In the view of a large portion of mainstream Christianity, Mormons not baptizing their infants might cause division in understanding, or outright "prove" that Mormons are not true Christians for diverging from infant baptism. However, the doctrinal evidence in the New Testament does not support this practice. Christ illustrated children's innocence when he stated that children "are as the kingdom of heaven" and they have no need for this saving ordinance since they are already saved. Mormons do hold the Christian view that baptism is necessary for salvation.

Finally, this chapter distinguishes the difference between the Latter-day Saint and the saints that Catholics revere and pray to. Like Catholics, Mormons also define the "saint" to mean "holy" or "set apart"; however, the LDS concept of a "saint" is not set apart or esteemed higher than other members of the Christian faith. The LDS usage of "saints" reflects the same usage of the term by Paul and other Apostles to address the body of the Church.

When you compare these examples of doctrine espoused by Mormons in relation to the New Testament to those preached by other branches of Christianity, it is perplexing that Mormons are often considered a cult while so many Christian sects continue to accept extra-biblical practices that are not historically parallel with the biblical text.

*"Give me my wives and my children."*

—Genesis 30:26

*"Nathan said . . . I gave thee thy master's house, and thy master's wives into thy bosom, and gave thee the house of Israel and of Judah."*

—2 Samuel 12:7–9

# 4
# More than One Wife?
## Plural Marriage

Red Flags and Misconceptions:

*The Bible teaches only one man and one wife.*
*Polygamy followed murder in the Bible (Genesis 4:19).*
*Deuteronomy 17 forbids plural marriage.*
*Old Testament practices are done away with.*
*The Book of Mormon teaches monogamy and contradicts LDS doctrine.*
*To repeal polygamy shows inconsistency within LDS belief.*

Probably the most infamous and misunderstood LDS doctrine—in this case a former practice—is plural marriage, or polygamy. While Latter-day Saints no longer practice plural marriage, there are those who still fault the Church for ever having accepted it. What those people do not understand is that at certain times and in certain circumstances, God himself prescribed the practice of plural marriage. The Church no longer practices plural marriage, but when it did, it was not inconsistent with biblical teachings.

With careful study, one will find that plural marriage both brought righteous benefits for God's people and wrought problems when men took multiples wives of their own will and in direct opposition to God's will.

**Old Testament: Polygamy Followed after Murder!**

In many of the early dispensations, holy and not-so-holy men practiced plural marriage. Plural marriage first surfaces in the Bible with the third generation from Cain—Lamech, a murderer (Genesis 4:23–24). According to Christian scholar H. H. Halley, "Polygamy soon followed murder, in Cain's family. God has ordained from the start, that one man and one woman live together in marriage. But soon man managed otherwise" (Halley, 70). Clearly, Halley portrays the practice of plural marriage as heinous and ungodly. Note that Halley says, "But soon *man* managed otherwise," meaning that man decided to change the definition of "marriage." Halley clearly suggests that any practice of plural marriage is man's doing. In contrast, the Lord gives his servant and prophet Abraham another wife in order to bear him a son because his first wife was barren (Genesis 16). Abraham's example is righteous, and the practice of plural marriage, when given by heavenly edict, is not considered adultery in God's eyes.

In Genesis 30, Jacob is in the service of his mother's brother, Laban. Laban promises Rachel to Jacob, but instead Jacob receives Leah, as it was a custom in their day to marry the eldest daughter first (Genesis 29:26). Jacob accepts the custom, but, determined to marry his true love, he works seven more years to receive his second wife, Rachel. Jacob is married to both and later marries two other women. Jacob—renamed "Israel" by the Lord—is a beloved prophet of God and the father of the House of Israel, the chosen people of God. The Lord again approves the practice of taking more than one wife in order to raise seed, establish the House of Israel, and to further the covenant given to Abraham.

In 2 Samuel 12, the Lord gives David his wives by the hand of the prophet Nathan, and all are righteous *except* in the case of Bath-sheba, the wife of Uriah. David became prideful and ordered Uriah to the front of a battle to ensure his death. This story gives an example of both a righteous case (plural marriage) and an unrighteous case (adultery). God approved the practice of plural marriage through his prophet but condemned the commission of adultery. One situation explains marriage by the hand of God's prophet, Nathan. The other clearly describes David's lust for another man's wife, in which he has Uriah killed to gain Bath-sheba's companionship.

## Turning Away Man's Heart: Deuteronomy 17 Condemns Plural Marriage

Critics often use the law given in Deuteronomy 17 as evidence of the unlawful practice of plural marriage and use this to rebut Mormon theology. Under the Law of Moses, Deuteronomy 17:17 states: "Neither shall he [the king] multiply wives to himself, that his heart turn not away: neither shall he greatly multiply to himself gold and silver."

Notice that the law provides the consequence of a king multiplying wives to himself—turning his heart away. Notice also that it emphasizes that the king is not to multiply such things on his own accord. Kings David and Solomon properly received their multiple wives as servants of God and by God's authority. However, this turning away of the heart occurred with King Solomon in 1 Kings 11, which says: "Strange women . . . ye shall not go in to them, neither shall they come in unto you: for surely they will turn away your heart after their gods: Solomon clave unto these in love." Again, as with Deuteronomy 17:17, the command to not multiply wives to one's self speaks in terms of wives from other nations, who would seek to turn the hearts of Israelites toward their false gods. The scriptures forbid Israelites to marry outside of the covenant people (Genesis 26:34–45; 1 Kings 11).

Another righteous example of plural marriage is described after the land of Israel is divided into Israel and Judah during the reigns of Abijah and Jeroboam. According to 2 Chronicles 13, Abijah is a righteous man who has the Lord on his side and who himself takes fourteen wives. The fact that Abijah serves God and is in good favor with the Lord further illustrates that God ordained plural marriage under circumstances that only he commands.

## The Old Testament Is Done Away With

Most critics argue that the covenant of the New Testament does away with the Law of Moses. They also assume several other Old Testament principles were made null and void, including temples and tithing. Christ, as the last sacrifice, did nullify the ancient temple practice of sacrificing the firstling of their flocks. Was this the case with plural marriage? The problem with attaching plural marriage to Old Testament practices like temple sacrifices is that plural marriage existed before the Law of Moses. Besides, within the New Testament, neither Christ nor his Apostles ever condemned the practice of plural marriage. Where then, without the New Testament, do critics look to for support to condemn the early Latter-day Saints?

## EARLY LDS PRACTICES

In Glen M. Leonard's book, *Nauvoo, A Place of Peace, A People of Promise* (343–347), he describes the conditions of early Latter-day Saints' experience with plural marriage.

To paraphrase, Leonard states that the Prophet Joseph Smith brought back the practice for reasons that were necessary in 1843. While studying the Old Testament and working on his translations of the Bible, this issue of polygamy stirred in Smith's mind. In answer to a prayer, the Lord revealed more truth on this misunderstood practice to Smith. He was told that one day the Latter-day Saints would have to practice it again. Joseph Smith was not the only one to ask the question after reading the Old Testament. Other saints came to Joseph Smith to get his advice on the doctrine. Joseph Smith made sure to let some of his members know that the day would come to bring back the ancient practice. That knowledge did not sit too well with some of them. Some would be disqualified from the practice because of immoral behavior. This was to be a practice that was respectable before God, not motivated by sexual pleasures.

A popular anti-Mormon claim refers to a quote by Brigham Young and tries to discredit current LDS beliefs because today Mormons have apparently diverged from Young's teachings. Critics argue that members not practicing plural marriage today will not receive exaltation (becoming like God or entering the highest level of heaven, explained in the next two chapters) because Brigham Young said, "The only men who become Gods, even the Sons of God, are those who enter into polygamy" (Journal of Discourses 11:268). However, he was speaking specifically in his time and to those he commanded, through his prophetic authority as in the days of old. In early LDS days, polygamy was again a conditional doctrine as it has always been; this was not a "doctrine or practice lawful for the whole church" (Leonard, 349). LeGrande Richards says in his book *A Marvelous Work and A Wonder* that "never over three percent" lived the practice, and "there must have been something of outstanding worth and conviction to hold 97 percent of the Church membership true to their testimonies" (Richards, 401).

## Is LDS doctrine contradictory concerning polygamy?

One may find, through an Internet search, that LDS scriptural teachings supposedly contradict one another. One scripture in Doctrine and Covenants section 132 opens up with the Lord saying that he "justified my servants Abraham, Isaac, and Jacob, as also Moses, David and Solomon, my servants, as touching the principle and doctrine of their having many wives and concubines." However, critics fail to read further where the principles and conditions of plural marriage are established in this section. Verse 38 says that David and Solomon took many wives, but "in nothing did they sin *save in those things which they received not of me*" (italics added). A key phrase from this verse—"save in those things which they received not of me"—supports the point made earlier: when men take multiple wives of their own will instead of through the direction of God, it is considered a sin. Notice in the section in 1 Kings 11:1–2 where it describes Solomon taking those "received not of me": "But King Solomon loved many strange women. . . . The Lord said unto the children of Israel, Ye shall not go in to them . . . for surely they will turn away your heart after their gods."

Among those who seek to criticize or point out contradictions within LDS scripture, Richard and Joan Ostling, authors of *Mormon America: The Power and the Promise*, claim that the Book of Mormon "was conventionally monogamous" (Ostling, 66). The Ostlings are correct in that it was not usual to find plural marriage in the Book of Mormon. For whatever reason, there are no good examples of the practice in the Book of Mormon, so it is mostly monogamous.

Another example from the Book of Mormon that seems to support the Ostlings' claim can be found in a statement from the Book of Mormon prophet Jacob: "Behold, David and Solomon truly had many wives and concubines, which thing was abominable before me, thus saith the Lord." It seems evident from that verse that the Lord is against plural marriage—if the statement were to stand alone. But this verse does *not* stand alone. We know, from the Bible and the Doctrine and Covenants, which of the wives that David and Solomon took were abominable (1 Kings 11 and 2 Samuel 12). However, Jacob does not go into all the details of David and Solomon's righteous wives given to them by the Lord, and rightfully so because Jacob is chastising the Nephites for their "grosser crimes" (Jacob 2:23). He does, however, say that the Nephites "understand not the scriptures" and explains the reason for plural marriage was to "raise seed" (verse 30). I'm convinced that the Ostlings, like these particular Nephites, erred in their understanding of the scriptures. They must have overlooked verse 30, like most do whose agenda it is to discredit Mormonism. With the combination of the righteous and unrighteous examples explained in all the scriptures, light has been shed on this apparent contradiction; Doctrine and Covenants 132 and Jacob 2 are actually consistent in their explanation. In cases like this, where scripture can remain silent on details we as readers presume are relevant, context makes all the difference.

Jacob (in the Book of Mormon) as well as Joseph Smith had an understanding of the dual nature of plural marriage, of the abominations, conditions, and righteous reasoning behind it. David and Solomon were in the wrong at times because they married outside of God's covenant people or, in David's case, committed murder and adultery. For covenant people to marry outside of the faith is a serious breach in God's eyes because it led the believer down the road to idolatry or accepting their spouse's false beliefs. The Bible is detailed on covenant marriages, but never once does God correct anyone for practicing plural marriage, unless—and *only* unless—it involves taking a wife without God's blessing or taking wives not of the covenant. However, the Bible also does not give men the authority to take multiple wives unless it's under the direction of his prophets. Deuteronomy 17 proclaims that kings are not to multiply wives unto themselves, but this fails as evidence against Mormonism because prophets (not kings) possess the authority to direct this practice. To critics loyal to the Bible, where does this leave them on the issue? The negative branding as a "polygamous cult" should be lifted from the association with Mormonism when the true nature of plural marriage is clearly communicated in this scriptural context.

## Conclusion

The Bible clearly describes cases of authorized plural marriage as well as cases where it was an abomination. To summarize, the following scriptures provide the needed context: Jacob 2:23–33, Doctrine and Covenants 132:39, 2 Samuel 12:7–9, and 1 Kings 11:2.

Having more than one wife by the Lord served as a practical option in extreme human circumstances, and God must afford a means to balance his positive laws (marriage) and sin (such as adultery). David and Solomon practiced unrighteous polygamy and were chastised for it, while Abraham and others practiced it in righteousness. This contrast brings a clearer understanding of plural marriage in its correct context, begging those who believe in the Old Testament but are critical of Mormonism to reconsider their position on the matter that early Mormons did not sin at the time they practiced it.

Finally, to clear up any ideas that repealing plural marriage shows contradictions or inconsistency in LDS doctrine, Elder Bruce R. McConkie explains:

> Plural marriage is not essential to salvation or exaltation. Nephi and his people were denied the power to have more than one wife and yet they could gain every blessing in eternity that the Lord ever offered to any people. In our day, the Lord summarized by revelation the whole doctrine of exaltation and predicated it upon the marriage of one man to one woman. (Doctrine and Covenants 132:1–28.) Thereafter he added the principles relative to plurality of wives with the express stipulation that any such marriages would be valid only if authorized by the President of the Church (Doctrine and Covenants 132:7, 29–66.) All who pretend or assume to engage in plural marriage in this day, when the one holding the keys has withdrawn the power by which they are performed, are guilty of gross wickedness. (McConkie, 578)

*"For this cause I bow my knees unto the Father of our Lord Jesus Christ, of whom the whole family in heaven and earth is named."*

—Ephesians 3:14–15

*"I ascend unto my Father, and your Father; and to my God, and your God.*

—John 20:16

# 5

# Man's Relationship to God

## Premortality and Man's Potential

Red Flags and Misconceptions:

*Mormons have no biblical evidence for premortal life.*
*Mormons believe Jesus and Lucifer were brothers.*
*God is without form.*
*There are no gods formed after God—only one God forever.*
*Mormons are polytheistic.*
*Mormons believe they will own their own planet.*

One characteristic of LDS theology that often sparks negative commentary or backlash from critics is the LDS perception of God: that Mormons say God has a body, that our spirits lived with God in a premortal existence, and that man has the potential to be like God. As an extension of their belief of the potential to be like God, Mormons are also viewed as polytheistic in worship. Polytheism is traditionally rejected by believers of the Old and New Testament who claim that there is only one God; Mormons also reject polytheism because the Father is supreme. This chapter focuses primarily on two of these distinct LDS doctrines that are seemingly hidden in the Bible: the premortal life and man's potential to become like God—in other words, life before life and the afterlife.

God having an immortal body of flesh and bone and the claim that Mormons are polytheistic will be expressed in this chapter in relation to the two other primary topics.

### Premortal Existence

To many Christians, the Mormon concept of premortal life seems to be extra-biblical. As summarized in the quote below, critics often reference the following verses to combat the idea of a premortal existence:

> Zechariah 12:1 that states, "The Lord, which stretcheth forth the heavens, and layeth the foundations of the earth, and formeth the spirit of man within him."
>
> 1 Corinthians 15:46 that says, "Howbeit that was not first which is spiritual, but that which is natural; and after that which is spiritual." (Sandra Tanner, "Terminology differences")

These act as a foundation to contest LDS doctrines on premortal life; critics claim that earth life is just a condition in which we as creatures are first given life and that life will cease unless we accept Christ as our Savior. I take the description "formeth the spirit of man within him" as a simple statement of fact: that God did form the spirit of man within him. This statement does not refute the idea that there was a premortal existence. Also, Paul is addressing the topic of resurrection in 1 Corinthians 15, and is not providing a dialogue that dismisses a premortal existence.

Both the Old and New Testaments provide several narratives about a premortal life where there was a host or family of heaven described. When God laid the foundations of the earth, all the sons of God shouted for joy, as recorded in Job 38:4–7. One-third of the *host of heaven* and Lucifer, *all of them angels*, were cast out of heaven for their wickedness (Isaiah 14:12–14; Jude 1:6). To the prophet Jeremiah, God acknowledges a preparatory period for the intelligences or spirits that God breathed into man when he says, "Before I formed thee in the belly I knew thee; and before thou camest forth out of the womb I sanctified thee, and I ordained thee a prophet unto the nations" (Jeremiah 1:5). In the New Testament (John 9:1–3), the disciples pass by a blind man and asked Christ to explain who had sinned—the man *before he was born* or his parents? Christ responded that "neither hath this man sinned, nor his parents; but that the works of God should be made manifest in him." One can assume, from the nature of this conversation, the disciples had a fundamental understanding of a pre-Earth life.

The Topical Guide in the KJV Bible organizes scriptures topically and allows the reader to make connections between various verses, as in this example of the "premortal life." For further biblical evidence of man's premortal state, the following verses below coupled with the narratives mentioned in Job, Isaiah, Jeremiah, and Jude build a strong foundation for the theology that man's spirit existed before mortality:

## VERSES ABOUT PREMORTAL LIFE FROM THE LDS SCRIPTURES' TOPICAL GUIDE:

### Old Testament

When God laid the foundations of the earth, all the sons of God shouted for joy (Job 38:4–7). The spirit shall return unto God who gave it (Ecclesiastes 12:7). Before I formed thee in the belly I knew thee (Jeremiah 1:4–5).

### New Testament

We are all his offspring (Acts 17:28). God chose us before the foundation of the world (Ephesians 1:3–4). We are to be in subjection to the Father of spirits (Hebrews 12:9). The angels which kept not their first estate, he hath reserved in everlasting chains (Jude 1:6; Abraham 3:26). The Devil and his angels were cast out (Revelation 12:9).

### Book of Mormon

They were called and prepared from the foundation of the world (Alma 13:3).

### Doctrine and Covenants

Christ looked upon the expanse of eternity and the hosts of heaven before the world was made (Doctrine and Covenants 38:1). Man was also in the beginning with God (Doctrine and Covenants 93:29; Helaman 14:17; Doctrine and Covenants 49:17). Noble spirits were chosen in the beginning to be rulers in the Church (Doctrine and Covenants 138:53–55). Many received their first lessons in the world of spirits (Doctrine and Covenants 138:56).

**Pearl of Great Price**

All things were created spiritually before they were on earth (Moses 3:5). I made the world, and men before they were in the flesh (Moses 6:51). Abraham saw the intelligences that were organized before the world was (Abraham 3:21–24). The life before earth life. All men and women lived with God as his spirit children before coming to the earth as mortal beings. This is sometimes called the first estate (Abraham 3:26).

From the perspective of the Bible as seen in these verses listed above, there can be no doubt that man possessed a spirit body in the premortal life. Again we see the Bible and other scriptures supporting a doctrine unique to the LDS Church.

### Jesus and Lucifer: Brothers?

Many critics feel that it is blasphemous to put their Lord in relation to the devil this way. The confusion about this belief arises when critics attempt to recite this doctrine to others, presuming that Mormons believe that the mortal Jesus Christ had a brother named Lucifer. While that presumption is grossly incorrect, both Jesus and the devil were known by different names in the biblical premortal existence—Jesus as Jehovah and Satan as Lucifer. Jesus is the name given to Jehovah while he performed his earthly ministry. In the premortal life, Lucifer was known as the "son of the morning" and lived in heaven as well before being cast out (Isaiah 14:12–14):

> How art thou fallen from heaven, O Lucifer, son of the morning! how art thou cut down to the ground, which didst weaken the nations! For thou hast said in thine heart, I will ascend into heaven, I will exalt my throne above the stars of God: I will sit also upon the mount of the congregation, in the sides of the north: I will ascend above the heights of the clouds; I will be like the most High.

This belief is predicated from the doctrine that all spirits are begotten of the Father and lived in the premortal existence together. Lucifer's once-esteemed status and fall from grace resemble other biblical characters. The prophet Adam's own son Cain rose up in jealousy of his brother Abel and slew him. The Apostle Judas Iscariot, once a trusted servant called personally by Christ to represent his church, fell from his position when he betrayed the Savior for thirty pieces of silver.

Did Lucifer and Jesus share a childhood in mortality? No. Once again, critics fail to see the underlying biblical narratives of the premortal family and Lucifer rising against his Father and being thrown out of the Kingdom.

### Does God Have a Body?

Does God possess a body? Mainstream Christianity teaches that God is not in bodily form but rather something too incomprehensible to imagine. God instructed that man be created in his own image; in Genesis 1:26 it says, "And God said, Let us make man in *our image*, after our likeness" (italics added). God himself provides the template of man's creation, that it would be the same as his own and that of his Son, Jesus Christ. Then in Genesis 2:7, he introduces the term "soul." God first created man, the corruptible material or the body, and then breathed into man the breath of life, or the spirit, and man became a living "soul" (Ecclesiastes 12:7). So a "soul" can be defined as the mortal or immortal union (after resurrection) of body and spirit. So shouldn't this lead the critic to believe that if man was created in God's image that both God and Jesus have a body just as Adam who they created?

Critics cite John 4:24 that says "God is a Spirit" to rebuke Mormon theology that God has a body. "Adopting the critics' reading of this verse leads to some strange conclusions if we are consistent. Deuteronomy 4:28 says that our God can see, eat and smell. Can an unembodied spirit do that? Deuteronomy 4:24 and Hebrews 12:29 say that God is a consuming fire, 1 Jn 1:5 says God is light, and 1 Jn 4:4, 16 says that God is love" (LDS FAIR, "Mormonism and the nature of God/God is a Spirit"). These examples from the Bible are evidence of God's characteristics but not of his form. To speak to this argument that God is a spirit and ignore other scriptural reference that refer to his image, then based on these verses, is God a fire? Is he a light? Is he love? Then is he just a spirit? With man having characteristics we associate as "human," we can take this evidence and understand God's nature of having a body since we are created in his image.

To be sure of what is man's interpretation and what is divine, consider the comments of a current LDS Apostle on the matter of Christ and the Father possessing bodies. In an LA Times article, LDS Apostle Elder Jeffrey R. Holland is quoted saying, "The idea of a flesh-and-blood God should not sound strange to Christians, who, after all, believe in the bodily birth and resurrection of Jesus" (Burke, *Are Mormons Christian?*).

Further, modern-day revelation through the prophet Joseph Smith in Doctrine and Covenants 130:22 on this topic says, "The Father has a body of flesh and bones as tangible as man's; the Son also; but the Holy Ghost has not a body of flesh and bones, but is a personage of Spirit. Were it not so, the Holy Ghost could not dwell in us." That the Father and Son, whose image we are made after, are housed in immortal bodies is again evidence that Joseph Smith's revelations continue to bring us back to the Bible and are not creations of a new religion, as the critics suppose. Thus the LDS Church can be synonymous with first-century Christianity and vice versa.

## Man's Potential

In LDS theology, what is probably considered by non-Mormons as the most unusual or unorthodox biblical view is of man's potential to become like God, or a god. In the LDS Church, gaining eternal life means to live as God the Father lives, to fulfill the purpose of mortality, to become like him and Christ, or to be one with them (John 17:21).

Understanding where and who the premortal spirits were before this life is fundamental to understanding eternal life or "godhood." This idea of men's and women's potential to become gods and goddesses is not completely foreign to Evangelical Christianity. The famous Evangelical Christian C. S. Lewis endorsed such an idea. He wrote:

> The command *Be ye perfect* is not idealistic gas. Nor is it a command to do the impossible. He is going to make us into creatures that can obey that command. He said (in the Bible) that we were 'gods' and He is going to make good His words. If we let Him—for we can prevent Him, if we choose—He will make the feeblest and filthiest of us into a *god* or *goddess*, dazzling, radiant, immortal creature, pulsating joy and wisdom and love as we cannot not imagine, a bright stainless mirror which reflects back to God perfectly

> (though, of course, on a much smaller scale) His own boundless power and delight and goodness. The process will be long and in parts very painful; but that is what we are in for. Nothing less. He meant what He said. (Lewis, *Mere Christianity*, 205–206)

Notice Lewis's use of the capital "G" for God and the lowercase "g" for gods and goddesses. LDS theology teaches we can become like God, but we do not replace him, nor do we worship one another or any other gods. Further, this section must be properly understood with the following in mind, taken from a 1978 *Ensign* article (LDS Church publication) entitled "I Have a Question":

> First of all, we know that God the Father and Jesus Christ are separate individuals, each having a distinct role. God the Father is the Supreme Being—no one in the Godhead is on a peer level with our Father in Heaven. Moses recorded an excellent scriptural statement on this subject: God explained to Moses that "mine Only Begotten is and shall be the Savior, for he is full of grace and truth; *but there is no God beside me*." (Moses 1:6; italics added)
>
> President Joseph F. Smith and his counselors explained that the phrase "there is no God beside me" meant "beside me, above me, or equal to me, or to be an object of worship." They added that "the sole object of worship, God the Eternal Father, stands supreme and alone, and it is in the name of the Only Begotten that we thus approach him." (See James R. Clark, Messages of the First Presidency, vol. 4, p. 270–271.)" ("I Have A Question," LDS.org)

In an attempt to refute that man can become like God, critics refer to Genesis 3:4–5 as evidence that such theology is satanic: "The serpent said unto the woman, Ye shall not surely die: For God doth know that in the day ye eat thereof, then your eyes shall be opened, and ye shall be as gods, knowing good and evil."

One critic, known only as the "Man from Modesto" on his online blog, suggests from this scripture, "Satan is the original teacher of men becoming like God" (Man from Modesto).

However, this interpretation fails to recognize what the Lord says in Genesis 3:22 in relation to the verse above: "The Lord God said . . . the man has become as one of us, to know good and evil."

Satan, while tempting Adam and Eve to disobey God, says, "Ye shall be as gods, knowing good and evil," but that in itself does not necessarily make the statement a lie; the devil often mixes truth with evil. However, since God also says, "Man has become as one of us, to know good and evil," it must be truth, because God is a God of truth. From God's observation that Adam and Eve now knew good and evil, he says they were "as gods," but they were not gods *yet.* In order for them to become so, God gives Adam and Eve commandments, an opportunity to become like him by choosing the better part, and the ability to die and, through the Savior, live again. To become like him, Adam and Eve have to know good from evil to eventually become gods. To say that Mormon theology is satanic because it teaches that man "shall be as gods" goes against further evidence in the Bible.

What does the Bible say about man's spirit in relationship to the Father and man's potential to become a god? It is necessary to note here the distinction between "man" as the biological and corruptible material and "man" as the essence or eternal spirit that dwells in the body—man's eternal self: his spirit, heart, and mind, with the goal of helping man achieve godhood through the Atonement of Jesus Christ. Table 5.1 provides numerous examples given in the Old and New Testaments that man's spirit has the potential to be exalted.

The Bible describes God as the God of gods, Christ asks men

**Table 5.1**
**Man's Spirit in Relationship with the Father**

| | |
|---|---|
| Genesis 1:26–27 | Made man in *his* image |
| Psalm 82:6 | Ye are gods, Children of the Most High |
| Psalm 136:2 | God of gods |
| John 10:34 | Ye are gods? |
| John 17:11, 21–23 | Becoming *one* in faith |
| Romans 8:14–17 | Children of God . . . joint-heirs with Christ |
| Hebrews 1:3 | Express image of his person |
| | **Modern Revelation** |
| Doctrine and Covenants 121:28 | Nothing shall be withheld, whether there be one God or many gods, they shall be manifest. |
| Doctrine and Covenants 132:20, 37 | Then shall they be gods; They are not angels but are gods |

to be one with him, and Paul says to the Romans that we may be joint-heirs with Christ and the Father. In Psalms, we learn two important characteristics of man: that they are called gods (they have the potential) and that they are the children of the Most High. Though man may become gods, nothing in LDS doctrine states that man is or will be equal to the Father. Contrary to critics of Mormon theology, Joseph Smith's teachings once again seek to restore originally Christian doctrine from the Bible.

### Are Mormons Polytheistic?

Critics often confuse Mormon theology as being polytheistic—worshipping more than one God. In relation to the idea that man can become a god, mainstream Christians mistake this doctrine as the belief that more than one God exists, and thus Mormonism is viewed as a polytheistic faith. The argument comes from the first great commandment given to the children of Israel, who transitioned from a polytheistic society in Egypt where multiple gods were worshipped. God gave to Moses the law that "thou shalt have no other gods before me" (Exodus 20:4). Man's potential to become like God is not in question here; rather, this commandment exhorts Israel to turn away from idol worship.

In LDS doctrine, the Lord reveals in Doctrine and Covenants 20:19 that the Almighty God "should be the only being who they should worship." Mormonism does not teach its members to pray to or revere anyone but the Eternal Father. Prayers offered to him are offered through his Son and our advocate, Jesus Christ.

In John 1:1, "the Word" is referred to as Christ, who (Christ) is with God, and is God (Christ). So Christ is separate from the Father (God), but his role as a god is asserted here in the phrase "the Word was with God"—Christ is one in purpose with God the Father. This verse seems to recognize a Father God having a Son who is also a god, and from John 17:21 we know they are both one in purpose.

The Bible clearly describes a multiplicity of Gods (in this case, two, being the Father and Christ); however, there is a hierarchy in this oneness, with the Father being the only God we are to worship. Man started as a spirit, and he progressed to mortality, where he was commanded to seek and take part in this "oneness" by living according to the true principles of the Gospel. If he can do so, "oneness" (with the Father and the Son) can be achieved in the next life—in other words, we can become gods and goddesses or heirs of "all that the Father hath" (Doctrine and Covenants 84:38).

### Timeout: The Bible Confirms Gods in the Beginning

Just like in John 1:1, where it describes Christ with the Father, in Genesis 3:22 it says, "man has become as one of us." Numerically, how many gods make "us"? Was this a conversation between Christ (Jehovah) and the Father? This plurality of gods speaking is reminiscent of God speaking to Abraham in Abraham 4:1—"Let *us* go down. And they went down at the beginning, and they, that is the *Gods*, organized and formed the heavens and the earth" (italics added).

### Early Christian Writers: Christ Is Distinct from the Father as an Individual

What is and is not "orthodox" Christianity has become a theme in this book. Some sources of ancient Christianity speak of the "subordination" of the Son to the Father. Christian historian Bettenson said that " 'Subordinationism' . . . was pre-Nicene orthodoxy," and Hippolytus, an early Christian writer, wrote that the Father is "the Lord and God and Ruler of all, and even of Christ Himself" (Bickmore, 118). Irenaeus, a priest of the Church of Lyons who lived in the second century AD, says, "Neither the prophets, nor the Apostles, nor the Lord Christ in His own person, did acknowledge any other Lord or God, but the God and Lord supreme. . . . The Father, is the only God and Lord, who alone is God and ruler of all" (Bickmore, 119). Clearly, before the Council at Nicaea many prominent Christian writers accepted that Christ was subordinate to his Father. The New Testament provides further details that distinguish the roles or authority between Father and Son. In Matthew 24:36, Christ affirms that only his Father knows of the second coming. In John 8:28–29 Christ says that "I can do nothing of myself; but as my Father hath taught me" and "The Father hath not left me alone; for I do always those things that please him." That the Son was subordinate to the Father was a well-known concept amongst the earliest Christians before the Council at Nicaea.

Here again, men in a different time used the same type of language found in LDS doctrines revealed through Joseph Smith to us in these modern times. In essence, saying there is more than "one god" crosses a fine line and does not sit well either with the critics of Mormonism or with how most Christians traditionally think of God. In my opinion, "God" almost appears to be a condition or title in which the Father, Son, and Holy Spirit exist as immortal, infinite, all-knowing, and pure beings. Man is given the potential and the command to become one with them, or gods, to share in this immortal and perfect condition. But God the Father will always remain supreme and the one whom we are commanded to worship.

## One God, No Idols

### Old Testament

Fundamental to Christianity, Islam, and Judaism is the belief that only one God exists. To counter the doctrine of men becoming gods, critics reference Isaiah 41–48 to prove their point of view that only one God exists, always and forever.

- 41:29—The Lord speaks against Idols.
- 42:8, 17—The Lord will not give his glory or praise to graven images, Israel shall be ashamed for trusting graven images.
- 43:10–15—The Lord speaks of himself as being the Israelite means of salvation, being the "only one."
- 44:10—Molten images are not profitable.
- 45:5—No God beside me, contrasted with verses 16, 20, and 22, talking of idols and that the Lord is their only salvation.
- 46:1—Idols are mentioned again.
- 48:12—"I am he, I am the first, I also am the last."

Mormons can agree, in the correct context of these Isaiah chapters, that God the Father and nothing else on earth is meant to be worshipped and that his Son is the only one who possesses the power to save souls. If one takes into consideration the background of those chapters in Isaiah, they will notice the people of Israel had a problem worshipping the false gods and molten images of other nations. Recall when Moses led the Israelites across the Red Sea and their worship of the golden calf as Moses descended with the Ten Commandments. The Lord, speaking singularly as he does throughout scripture, makes it clear that the Almighty God provides the means of salvation and these other "gods" have no power to save them.

To use these verses against the eternal perspective in place of the context of rebuking false idol worship—and to believe doing so counters the belief that God's children can become like he is—runs counter to the New Testament.

### New Testament

In 1 John 3:2, John says, "Now are we the sons of God, and it doth not yet appear what we shall be: but we know that, when he shall appear, we shall be like him, for we shall see him as he is." Men and women who followed Christ in the flesh and lived true to their covenants shall be like God, because man will be resurrected, live forever, attain an immortal body as the Savior did, and be a joint-heir with Christ, thus receiving all that the Father has (John 16:15, Romans 8:17, 32; Revelation 21:7; Doctrine and Covenants 84:38). Because Mormons believe they can become a god and "receive all that the Father hath," critics use foreign language like "owning their own planet" to dismiss this idea and classify the LDS Church as a cult.

The Apostle Paul says, "As there be gods many, and lords many, to us there is only one God" (1 Corinthians 8:5). What is Paul saying? Does this mean man does not have the potential to become like God, because there is only one? Who or what are these "gods" and "lords" Paul speaks of? Earlier in the same chapter, Paul sets the context of his preaching by referencing idolatry. Another reference where Paul is rebuking idol worship can be found in Acts 17:22–28; speaking to the Greeks in the midst of Mars Hill, he says:

> Ye men of Athens, I perceive that in all things ye are too superstitious. For as I passed by, and beheld your devotions, I found an altar with this inscription, TO THE UNKNOWN GOD. Whom therefore ye ignorantly worship, him declare I unto you. God that made the world and all things therein, seeing that he is Lord of heaven and earth, dwelleth not in temples made with hands. . . .

> For in him we live, and move, and have our being; as certain also of your own poets have said, For we are also his offspring.

Paul continues to speak of "One God" in terms of worship and rebuking the worship of false idols, but he also emphasizes our divine nature and our being's potential spiritual progression, as do Isaiah and other teachers in the Bible.

When put in context, it becomes clear that scriptures referenced by LDS critics fail to argue the point against LDS teachings on the plurality of Gods and have everything to do with false idol worship. If there is a question of there being more than one God, LDS theology is consistent with what God promises man as his reward and with the doctrine that only the Father is to be worshipped.

## Conclusion

Did man exist before this life? The Bible clearly states that when God "laid the foundations of the earth," the sons of God "shouted for joy at the creation of the world." Further, it states that our spirits "will return to the Father who gaveth." There are other examples throughout biblical text that support the theology of a pre-earth life where spirits were with God before mortality began. These references answer the age-old question man has always wondered: "Where did we come from?"

From earlier discussion, we know that all of Heavenly Father's offspring are related as part of one heavenly family, and as part of that family, we learn that Jesus and Lucifer were brothers in the premortal existence. As learned in the scriptures, some of these children—as seen in the examples of Cain and Judas the betrayer—were once esteemed beings who became fallen through their disobedience to God their Father. While Lucifer and Jesus were not mortal brothers, this parallel relationship can be understood in relation to the premortal existence of man.

Mainstream Christians assert that God is everywhere and without form. The Old Testament describes God the Father as having human characteristics such as seeing, hearing, and eating. This argument is further strengthened by his Son's appearance to the apostles, who felt his wounds and witnessed his ascension into heaven in his glorified and immortal, tangible body. There is a consensus between the Old and New Testaments that God has a body and is not just a spirit.

LDS doctrine teaches that God created "worlds without end," that we are to worship and believe in one God, that the Father is the Supreme Being of the universe, and that Jesus is his literal offspring (Acts 17:29). Jesus was sent to do the will of the Father and is in fact our brother. His special mission to die for the sins of all mankind was given to him before the foundation of the world (1 Peter 1:20). He is now exalted with a perfect, immortal body of flesh and bones and stands on the right hand of the Father. He is also Jehovah of the Old Testament. Christ is Jehovah; he created this world and all things in and around it. He did this at the will of the Father. The LDS doctrine of man's potential is dually consistent with the Old Testament worship of the one true God and the New Testament teaching wherein Christ says we can be "joint heirs" and *be as he is* with the Father: one.

So are Mormons polytheistic? I have shown it is not so easy to create labels like this with the biblical text. Do Mormons believe they will be gods one day or, in the critics' terminology, "own their own planet"? If the idea of monotheism dominates the religious conversation and thus brands Mormons for their belief that man can become a god, it can immediately create a wall between Mormonism and other truth seekers. Understanding that Mormons are similar in their worship of only one God, God the Father as the Supreme Being, this barrier can be overcome. Thus, religious historians have limited scriptural understanding of a definition that falsely brands Mormonism as polytheistic without recognizing that their belief systems of the worship of one Supreme Being are similar to that of Mormons, who they hesitate to recognize as Christian. This chapter has revealed several biblical descriptions of false idol worship in contrast with the Lord saying that God is the only God and only through him do they have salvation. The term "one God" in this context is only referring to the worship of idols and images, such as the golden calf. Joseph Smith's revelation from God helped bring to light scriptures that had been overlooked or forgotten and revealed God's purpose of man's potential to become like him and inherit "all that he hath."

Finally, the Bible's descriptions of a premortal man's relationship to God and man's potential to become like him are consistent with

God's intent for man to understand the purpose of his existence. The question often asked throughout the ages—"Why are we here?"—is answered as we come to understand God and man's relationship with him as well as man's potential as a child of the Almighty God.

*"There is one glory of the sun, and another of the moon,
and another of the stars; for one star differeth from another star in glory.
So is also the resurrection of the dead."*

—1 Corinthians 15:41–42

6

# The Afterlife and Salvation

## One Heaven and One Hell, or Three Degrees of Glory?

Red Flags and Misconceptions:

*Belief in an afterlife was introduced later in religion, not through the divine.*

*There is only one heaven and one hell.*

*Either you are saved or you go to hell.*

In the previous chapter, the misconception that Mormons are polytheistic or that they will own their own planet was discussed in light of what the Bible says about man's potential. The focus in this chapter continues from the previous chapter of man reaching his full potential on earth and receiving reward or glory in the hereafter. It may be surprising to many religious thinkers that the belief in an afterlife has been questioned by secular historians who propose that Christianity and the Bible borrowed the idea of an afterlife from neighboring cultures.

### The Bible and an Afterlife

Historians point out that much of the Bible seems silent on the afterlife and the resurrection. Recall the great blessing God gave

Abraham, to be "a father of many nations" and given "the land of Canaan, for an everlasting possession" (Genesis 17:5, 8). Historian Kevin Reilly deciphers these verses to mean "there is no heaven—no afterlife. God promised Abraham land and prosperity, not an afterlife. Even today, a belief in personal immortality is more accepted by Christians than Jews." Reilly suggests that what was the ancient Hebrew faith system evolved into Judaism, which in time spawned Christianity, and that religion continuously transforms from its religious parental roots (Reilly, 219). Surely there are references to resurrection or an afterlife throughout the Bible. Could the faith system of the Bible simply be an idea that has evolved over time to suit the interests of those changing it, or is there another answer?

In the story of the Garden of Eden, recorded in Genesis 3:22, perhaps we find the beginnings of an answer:

> And the Lord God said, Behold, the man is become as one of us, to know good and evil: and now, lest he put forth is hand, and take also of the tree of life, and eat, and live forever: Therefore the Lord God sent him forth from the garden of Eden, to till the ground.

That a "tree of life" exists in this early biblical telling implies the potential to live forever could have been an option for Adam and Eve. However, God decides to appoint death upon his children and commands them to "multiply and replenish the earth" to roll out the plan for his children to live in mortality and gain experience.

Other examples illustrate that knowledge of an afterlife existed among ancient Hebrews. In 1 Samuel 2:6 it says "The Lord killeth, and maketh alive: he bringeth down to the grave, and bringeth up." Job 14:10, 13–14 poses the question, "If a man die, shall he live again?" and describes man giving up the ghost. Job also says that "all the days of my appointed time will I wait, till my change come." Continuing in Job 19:25: "For I know that my redeemer liveth, and that he shall stand at the latter day upon the earth: And though after my skin worms destroy this body, yet in my flesh shall I see God."

The prophet Isaiah, in Isaiah 25:8–9, says, "He will swallow up death in victory" and "we will be glad and rejoice in his salvation." The prophet Daniel in 12:2 says, "And many of them that sleep in the dust of the earth shall awake, some to everlasting life, and some to shame and everlasting contempt."

The verses are conclusive that a belief in an afterlife existed in the Hebrews' traditions and faith. As evidence that the Hebrews first acknowledged or declared their belief in the afterlife, Reilly suggests that this verse in Daniel is the first time a belief in an afterlife enters the Hebrew tradition. Reilly concludes that the Persians, neighbors to the Hebrews, were to credit for this belief's adoption into the Old Testament. For Reilly to limit a specific doctrine's origin to the latter books in the Old Testament ignores what Hebrews before Daniel clearly possessed in their writings. The references listed above clearly indicate the acknowledgement of an afterlife and heaven in the earliest stages of the Bible.

Why do historians miss these other references? Is their interest more geared toward portraying the Bible as something created solely by man rather than with God's influence? Historians do not look at the "written word" coupled with what would have been the "spoken word." For example, perhaps Moses spoke aloud to the Israelites from the book Genesis where it talks about the tree of life. Isaiah could have read from 1 Samuel 2:6 saying that "The Lord killeth, and maketh alive: he bringeth down to the grave, and bringeth up." To assume that the idea of an afterlife began later in the Hebrew tradition rejects what was known and recorded before the book of Daniel.

In light of the Restoration, we can easily relate that the biblical people possessed both the written and the spoken word and that their verbal dialogue is impossible to know. It is safe to say that these seemingly insignificant descriptions of an afterlife—well before the book of Daniel was written and hypothetically "influenced by Persians"—show that the people of the Bible possessed these nuggets of truth to verbally discuss. So was the idea adopted by Christians to appeal to social needs as historians might suggest, or was the idea there all along? From the Bible, it is evident that the idea of an afterlife existed beneath the surface from the beginning.

### Three Degrees of Glory

One hallmark of the Christian faith is the belief that, after living a Christian life, an eternal reward awaits in the life to come. An area where Mormons are not so different from mainstream Christianity is the belief in heaven and hell. However, LDS theology elaborates further through modern revelation given to Joseph Smith with the belief that there are three degrees of Heaven. Before the foundation of this world, the Father laid out a plan for his children to be tested and to return home in a condition that depends upon their individual effort and dedication to build his kingdom. Christ mentions that there are many mansions, or places set aside for all, perhaps because all of us are different and will choose to live different levels of devotion. The Mormon belief teaches that heaven is divided into three "glories," as Paul stated in 1 Corinthians 15:41–42 (see chapter heading). But mainstream Christianity preaches that there is one heaven and one hell, and this "all or nothing" belief directly contrasts the teachings of Paul.

The celestial kingdom is symbolized as the sun, the terrestrial kingdom as the moon, and the telestial kingdom as the stars. In Matthew 13:43 it says, "Then shall the righteous shine forth *as the sun* in the kingdom of their Father." This verse symbolizes the highest degree of glory, the celestial kingdom, where the righteous will dwell with God. This is also another name for "eternal life," living with God and like God.

Below are more detailed descriptions from Doctrine and Covenants 76 of the three kingdoms of heaven, outer darkness (perdition), and those who will inherit one of these kingdoms as the state of their salvation.

**Celestial**—These people received a testimony of Jesus, believed on his name and were baptized, and received all his ordinances. They kept his commandments and received the Holy Spirit by the laying on of hands by one who has been ordained. They are those whom the Father has given all things; they are gods, even the sons and daughters of God, and are risen in the first resurrection. They are those whose names are written in heaven, righteous men made perfect, and receive the highest of all glories, the glory of the sun.

**Terrestrial**—These people died without the law. Their spirits were kept in prison until the Son visited and preached the gospel to them; they did not receive a testimony of Jesus in the flesh, but afterwards received it. They are those who were honorable men who were blinded by the craftiness of men and did not receive the presence of the Father, or they are those who gained a testimony but were not valiant in their testimony of Jesus, and received a glory of the moon. Further clarification is given, as these believers have a firm testimony of Jesus Christ but will not accept baptism and the fulness of the gospel. "Knowledge and acceptance of the gospel is not necessary for having a testimony of the divinity of Jesus Christ" (Robinson and Garrett, *A Commentary On The Doctrine and Covenants*, Volume 2, 316).

**Telestial**—These are people who didn't receive the gospel of Christ, or a testimony of Jesus, but who did not deny the Holy Spirit. They are redeemed at the last resurrection and receive the glory of the stars.

**Outer Darkness**—These people denied the Son after the Father revealed him to them; in other words, they had a testimony but turned away in rebellion. They dwell with the devil and his angels and suffer endless torment of conscience.

Listed below are further evidences of biblical support that there is a separation within heaven of the different degrees of glory that man has the potential to attain.

**Table 6.1**
**New Testament Teachings on Resurrection and Glory**

| | |
|---|---|
| John 14:2 | "In my Father's house are many mansions." |
| The Acts 24:15 | "That there shall be a resurrection of the dead, both of the just and unjust" |
| 1 Corinthians 15:40–42 | "Sun, moon, stars . . . so also is the resurrection" |
| Hebrews 11:35 | "Obtain a better resurrection" |

Aside from the three glories of heaven and outer darkness (which are eternal in nature), there are two other temporary realms for the spirits of man after death called "spirit prison" and "paradise." Christ visited the spirit prison during the three days after his crucifixion to preach his gospel to those long dead (1 Peter 3:19–20, 4:6). Christ also mentioned this paradise to the thief while on the cross (Luke 23:43). Understanding that these two realms exist as described in Peter and Luke sheds light on other biblical accounts pertaining to the conditions of salvation. Mormons believe these realms exist for the purpose of preaching, just as Christ did before his resurrection, his gospel to the dead who did not have the opportunity to hear it while they were living on earth. Joseph Smith stated, "It is not all to be comprehended in this world; it will be a great work to learn our salvation and exaltation even beyond the grave" (Joseph Smith, *Teachings of the Prophet Joseph Smith*, 348). This preaching to the dead correlates with those who are deceased having the opportunity for accepting or rejecting the opportunity to learn and, further, make covenants with God.

### One Heaven and One Hell?

Among mainstream Christian belief, the final resting place for souls lies in either heaven or hell. Generally, throughout the Bible, and even in the Book of Mormon, these are mentioned as the only reward or punishment after death. However, biblical support and revelation given to Joseph Smith offer more specific details of what glories beyond heaven or hell God revealed to his prophets. In 2 Corinthians 12:2, Paul describes the "third heaven," though only a vague understanding can be taken from what Paul means. This may be because the Bible was translated from Hebrew to Greek and then to English, and some of the original meanings were lost. Other resources and further clarification are needed to help us understand this topic. This is why the spoken word of present-day revelation from God is necessary to clarify these teachings.

Some religions have the attitude that "if you are not ______ (fill in the blank with a religion), then you are not going to heaven." Who could possibly know for sure where one will end up in the afterlife? Such claims cause truth seekers to question, and give God and faith a bad rap. It is no wonder that irreligion is growing and people want no part of traditional religion. Revelation given to the Prophet Joseph Smith provided clarification on this complex issue and shed light on the Bible, revealing that the final judgment is not as exclusive as joining a traditional Christian congregation as some may assume. Recall the words of Paul in 1 Corinthians 15: "So also is the resurrection of the dead;" a glory of the sun, moon, and stars—all different from one another in their brightness—describes the resurrection. Apply that verse to the final judgment as Paul describes, and it becomes clear that God judges and mercifully provides a state of glory to all of his children following the resurrection.

But what is hell? For many Christians, the symbolism of "lake of fire," "brimstone," and "eternal torment" offer an uneasy picture of an eternity of endless suffering after death. Is there a literal "lake of fire," or is it a metaphor for an eternity wracked with an uncomfortable conscience? In my opinion, the fire as described in scripture symbolizes living in eternity with the knowledge that one could have attained a better resurrection. In LDS theology, neglecting to change a bad habit or viewing one's negative thoughts and actions as the norm may deny one further character growth—growth toward *being one with God*. Not being one with God could be considered "hell," knowing that it was possible to "have all that he hath" for eternity. To put it another way, such souls have their eternal progress dammed like a river, blocked from further glory. Imagine receiving an average resurrection, like one with the glory of the stars or moon as opposed to one as bright as the sun.

Mormons refer to the mainstream Christian idea of hell as "outer darkness" or "perdition." To get to this destination, it is understood that one must have had a full knowledge and testimony of Christ, only then to turn his or her back on Christ in a life of sin (Doctrine and Covenants 76). This final destination is for the spiritually dead, meaning that all good things have no value to them, and they detest good unsympathetically. "Hell" in another sense can also be described as the eternal knowledge one will carry in the next life knowing that attaining a higher glory was possible, as described in the previous paragraph.

According to LDS Apostle Bruce R. McConkie, the *salvation* referred to in Doctrine and Covenants 6:13 is "the salvation which the Saints seek" (McConkie, *Mormon Doctrine*, 670) and which the scriptures mostly speak of; not "basic salvation" (saved from death) but eternal life (the highest degree of glory). Recall that all are saved from death, both the just and the unjust, so even from the Bible two general types of salvation are plainly manifest.

### Early Christian Writers

Early Christian theologians acknowledged the degrees of glory following the judgment of man. Barry Bickmore quotes from a few of their writings. John Chrysostom (AD 347–407), a Christian bishop and preacher from the fourth and fifth centuries in Syria and

Constantinople, spoke of the "degrees of reward" in the afterlife: "That although they be all in God's Kingdom, all shall not enjoy the same reward; and though all sinners be in hell, all shall not endure the same punishment" (Bickmore, 240). Irenaeus referenced Christ who said, "In My Father's house are many mansions . . . who supplies all with a suitable dwelling-place" (Bickmore, 240). Early Christian theologian Clement of Alexandria, from the second century, echoed descriptions similar to that of the section 76 of the Doctrine and Covenants. Clement says, "There are various abodes, according to the worth of those who have believed . . . which are three, indicated by the numbers of the Gospel—the thirty, the sixty, the hundred" (Bickmore, 241). By what scriptural basis, as with the case of plural marriage, do "mainstream Christians" dismiss such Christian doctrine so easily?

## Conclusion

Biblical evidence is seen throughout both the Old and New Testaments to support the teaching of an afterlife and receiving reward or glory. While this teaching might have been seen throughout other cultures, it is clearly an original teaching to the children of Israel, with its roots leading back to Adam and Eve. Learning that there is organization and order to the afterlife depending on the degree of valiance to the knowledge of the gospel of Jesus Christ leads the believer to understand more fully the degrees of heaven and its different distinctions.

What does the Bible say of there being only one heaven and one hell? As mortals we are headed every day toward immortality, and it is our choices that shape our character, whether they be more toward God or away from him. Over and over again, the scriptures talk about heaven or hell, saved or not saved, eternal life or the lake of fire, and so forth. Many mainstream Christians unapologetically believe that if one does not accept their idea of Jesus, they are bound to hell.

LDS author LeGrand Richards said it best when he described the attitudes of those with the "one heaven, one hell" view. He says,

> This thought has led many to feel that while their lives may not be all they should be, they are as good as, or better than, the average.

> If this doctrine were true, it is obvious that a line would have to be drawn somewhere, and the closer one came to the line the less would be the difference or distinction between those who would cross the line and enter heaven and those who would not quite qualify, and therefore would be sent to hell. Such a doctrine does not have a motivating and stimulating power to impel or encourage men to do the best they can, but rather to satisfy themselves by doing as well as the average man. Such a doctrine places no value on anything more than average devotion and obedience to the commandments of the Lord, or the development of one's talents and their useful devotion to his service. (Richards, 253)

And what is salvation? Typically when the scriptures talk about "salvation," Latter-day Saints understand it to mean "returning home to the Father or attaining the highest degree of heaven." Though there are lesser degrees that one can attain, the scriptures always speak to believers who seek this higher kingdom. If Christ had said there was only one heaven and hell, then the scriptures would have made that known. However, he clearly states that man will be judged according to his works, and that there are many mansions.

*"Faith without works is dead."*

—James 2:26

*"They were judged every man according to their works."*

—Revelation 20:12

# 7

# SALVATION

## SAVED BY WORKS OR GRACE?

RED FLAGS AND MISCONCEPTIONS:

*By faith you are saved, not by works.*
*Mormons are saved by works, not by Christ.*
*Mormons add to Christ's sacrifice.*

Aside from the selling of indulgences, Martin Luther and other reformers came to reject many of the Catholic interpretations, rites, and works. The importance of grace through Christ seemed to escape the doctrine and dialogue in their day. Protestants directed their traditions toward the message of grace alone. No amount of work we do can save our souls—only the blood of Christ and his sacrifice. Whether our works or grace alone saves us has been highly debated for over 500 years. This point brings many Christians to contend with Mormons on the doctrine of salvation, because LDS theology emphasizes certain works—such as baptism, tithing, and temple covenants—and stresses that certain things must be "worked out" or learned to attain the highest degree in heaven.

### Do Mormons Rely More on Works than on Christ for Salvation?

Mormon critics believe that the LDS faith relies too much on works and ignores grace. In a 2011 BYU devotional, Brad Wilcox illustrated the different perspectives between Mormons and mainstream Christians on this topic:

> I have born-again Christian friends who say to me, "You Mormons are trying to earn your way to heaven."
>
> I say, "No, we are not earning heaven. We are *learning* heaven. We are preparing for it (see Doctrine and Covenants 78:7) . . . They ask me, "Have you been saved by grace?"
>
> I answer, "Yes. Absolutely, totally, completely, thankfully—yes!" Then I ask them a question that perhaps they have not fully considered: "Have you been *changed* by grace?" They are so excited about being saved that maybe they are not thinking enough about what comes next. They are so happy the debt is paid that they may not have considered why the debt existed in the first place." (Wilcox, *His Grace Is Sufficient*)

LDS theology teaches essential "works" that guide members down the straight and narrow path through mortality. If works are entirely unnecessary, how can a Christian who is "saved" in any number of the mainstream sects understand or accomplish their duty in this life? For example, to feed the hungry or build their character in a way that shows appreciation for and acceptance of the Lord's will. Teaching or emphasizing good works is to teach the Gospel of Christ. Christ spoke to the importance of good works in his Sermon on the Mount and to their purpose when he stated, "Let your light so shine before men, that they may see your good works, and glorify your Father which is in heaven" (Matthew 5:16).

In this argument as to whether the grace of God, good works, or both save us, critics miss the direct relation between the LDS emphasis on works and a love of and faith in God, obedience to him, and emulation of the words of Christ. It is not as if Mormons carry a checklist of daily good works to perform like some critics might have people believe. The Church has programs known as home teaching and visiting teaching as tools for outreach (or fellowship) toward all members. Other than that, there is no mysterious list of "good works" that Mormons must perform if they wish to receive salvation. Good works in LDS theology add up to good living, avoiding or overcoming addiction, being charitable, performing religious ordinances such as baptism, and treating others with small acts of kindness.

If LDS theology is to be condemned for emphasizing good works in conjunction with faith, consider what the New Testament says about good works in the following verses (Table 7.1) and what characteristics are expectations for discipleship.

**Table 7.1**
**New Testament and Good Works**

| | |
|---|---|
| Matthew 5:16 | "That they may see your good works" |
| John 13:15 | "For I have given you an example, that ye should do as I have done to you." |
| Romans 2:10 | "To every man that worketh good" |
| Ephesians 2:10 | "Good works . . . that we should walk in them" |
| Colossians 1:10 | "Being fruitful in every good work" |
| The Book of Titus | Most of this book deals with "good works" |
| James 2:24 | "By works a man is justified, and not by faith alone" |
| James 2:26 | "Faith without works is dead" |
| Revelation 20:12 | "They were judged every man according to their works" |

## Do Mormons Believe Christ's Sacrifice to Be Insufficient?

Critics often refer to 2 Nephi 25:23 (in the Book of Mormon), which states "that it is by grace that we are saved, after all we can do," to indicate that Mormons "add" to what Jesus did on the cross. For critics to say Mormons believe that Christ's sacrifice was insufficient is misleading and does not fully taken into account what the Bible says. The Bible tells us to "*work out our own salvation* with fear and trembling" (Phillipians 2:12, italics added). In Colossians 1:10, Paul says to the saints, "Ye might walk worthy of the Lord unto all pleasing, being fruitful in every good work, and increasing in the knowledge of God." Both Bible verses allude to the fact that salvation includes some effort on the individual's part.

## Repentance

It is possible for everyone to achieve the highest degree of glory through repentance. True repentance is taking the steps to change whatever bad habits or lifestyle choices are contrary to the laws of God. Certainly there are more sinful lifestyles that take a more severe toll on one's soul. God offers a path to repentance by acknowledging that, as humans, we sin. Romans 3:23 says, "For all have sinned, and come short of the glory of God." In order to repent, we must admit our sin is wrong, have sincere sorrow that our sin offends God, confess our sin to the Lord and (if necessary) to one of his representatives, and finally forsake the sin completely. Typically, Latter-day Saints look to their local bishops for guidance on more severe matters, while they look to the Lord for matters they feel they can work out with him on their own. Serious sins can lead a Latter-day Saint to face a counsel, "probation," temporary disfellowship, or, in the worst case, excommunication.

"Sin" is anything contrary to the laws of God, and while Mormons teach the importance of good works, they don't teach that salvation comes through works of the law (see Galatians 2:16). Mormons teach faith in Christ, and with this faith, good works should be the result. Having faith in Christ is a personal thing, and with Mormons, as well as with any group, some lose this relationship as they choose the things of the world rather than the things of God. If Mormons relied solely on the works of the law without faith, what would get rid of their guilt for sin? The central focus for the repentance process in LDS theology is faith in the grace of God and the Atonement of Christ, followed by total repentance. This is what Christ's gospel is all about: his plan to guide his sons and daughters home.

God's plan throughout mortality will not always be free of opposition, sorrow, heartache, and sin. The Father meant for these experiences to give us growth, hope, and opportunities to "overcome the world." In John 16:33, Christ says, "These things I have spoken unto you, that in me ye might have peace. In the world ye shall have tribulation: but be of good cheer; I have overcome the world." Human faults, then, are learning experiences and times to bow in humble prayer to God. The Lord's Supper, or the sacrament, allows a renewal of the covenants members made at baptism to forsake the evils that bring us pain and that provide only temporary pleasure. The sacrament is our privilege to gain weekly spiritual strength, for individuals to reflect on the previous week, and for the purpose of overcoming any sinful activities or habits to prevent further spiritual decline and to grow from those choices.

### All Are to Be Resurrected and Judged

The major sects differ from one another as to whether works and grace secure salvation, or grace alone. Both agree that God will separate the righteous from the sinners in the final judgment, sending souls to one eternal hell or one eternal heaven. Mormonism contends that the Bible elaborates further and that heaven is just as Paul described, with its three degrees of glory—that some will inherit all, be joint-heirs with Christ, and have all that the Father has, while others may fall short of that and inherit a portion of this glory (moon or the stars).

Through the Atonement of Jesus Christ, all will stand at judgment and attain a purchased state of basic salvation through his grace. This parallels what the Bible says: "As in Adam all die, even so in Christ shall all be made alive" (1 Corinthians 15:22). All mankind, whether they believe in God or not, will rise into immortality and be judged by their works and the desires of their hearts. In LDS theology, "eternal life" is being joint-heirs with Christ or being a god (attaining the highest degree of glory), while "salvation" can generically mean to inherit one degree of glory.

Contrary to critical assertions against the LDS Church, God provides a series of New Testament "works," including baptism, fellowship, charity, marriage, and obedience to God's commandments, to name a few. Those who are presented these options or teachings in life can choose to reject them, but God is bound to his covenants and rewards those who love and obey him. In this way, both God's mercy and justice are reflected in the arrangement of the degrees of heaven.

### Thief on the Cross: Salvation without Works?

Some believe that once they are "saved," they are on the path to heaven no matter what. Others believe that a simple, vocal acknowledgement of accepting Christ as their savior sanctifies them with his grace and they need do nothing more. What is written in the scriptures on this matter? One example critics make against the LDS emphasis on works for salvation is the story in which Christ promises the thief on the cross to be in "paradise" with him. In the story, the thief rebukes the other criminal who criticizes Christ for not being able to save himself, and in light of this, Christ acknowledges the thief's good heart and says, "Today shalt thou be with me in paradise" (Luke 23:43). Critics use this verse to presume that the moment one acknowledges Christ as their savior, even if on their deathbed—or in this case, a cross—eternal life is granted whether or not a deathbed confessor has received the required earthly ordinances (such as baptism), and regardless of whether they ever learned and lived the commandments of God. However, in John 3:5 it says, "Except a man be born of water and of the Spirit, he cannot enter into the kingdom of God." In Matthew 28:19 the Savior instructs the apostles to teach and baptize all in the name of the Father, and of the Son, and of the Holy Ghost.

Luke 23:43 says the thief on the cross was caught up to paradise. "Paradise," as mentioned in the previous chapter, describes a place where man resides after death and before resurrection and is given the opportunity to hear Christ's gospel. What does this mean? This is important because in LDS doctrine, all people who receive(d) the opportunity must act in faith and perform the proper ordinances to obtain eternal life: repentance, baptism, temple work (baptism for the dead), and so forth. Again, other believers outside of LDS understanding believe these works are unnecessary and use this story of the thief as their argument that only faith is necessary.

Some believe the thief went to the very heaven in which the Father dwells, but how can that be when Christ told the thief that they would be in paradise together? Jesus said he would be with the thief, yet when Jesus later appeared to Mary, he told her not to touch him because he had not yet been to his Father. If Christ had not yet been to the Father, the "paradise" that the thief was promised refers to what the Latter-day Saints teach as "paradise," or the "spirit world." Critics do not recognize the nature of the Savior's promise to the thief, believing instead that the thief went straight to heaven. But according to LDS belief, no one enters into the degrees of glory—the actual heaven—until the final judgment and resurrection. Until then, people go to the temporary spirit paradise or prison.

The thief had two places he could have gone—spirit paradise or prison—as explained by Peter, who described where Jesus was during the three days after his crucifixion:

> By which also he went and preached *unto the spirits in prison*; Which sometime were disobedient, when once the longsuffering of God waited in the days of Noah, while the ark was a preparing, wherein few, that is, eight souls were *saved by water.* (1 Peter 3:19–20, italics added)
>
> For this cause was the gospel preached also to them that are dead, that they might be judged according to men in the flesh, but live according to God in the spirit. (1 Peter 4:6)

"Paradise" as described in Revelations 2:7 seems more like a description of heaven and likely not used in the same context as was the story of the thief on the cross. The word "paradise" is only used three times. Other terms such as "throne," "kingdom of heaven," "heavens," and so on are used much more to describe what little the Bible says about heaven or the "heavens." These two verses do not do much for the critic's argument. The facts have been stated: Jesus had not yet been to the Father (John 20:17), so the thief could not have been either (Luke 23:43). If Jesus was in paradise, it would have been spirit paradise and prison where souls await resurrection (as described by Peter), as opposed to his Father's dwelling place.

## Conclusion

Are men saved by grace alone, or are works necessary to express faith and show appreciation to Christ for his sacrifice? If salvation, or eternal life, comes through baptism (and similar works), is motivated by faith, and is given to us by grace, it then appears to imply that Christ indeed requires more from us than a verbal acknowledgement that he died for us. If the Bible describes the resurrection as applying to both the just and the unjust, obtaining a glory of the sun, moon, or stars, and states that everyone will be judged according to their works, the concept of salvation is clearly much more involved than simply defining salvation as achievable by grace alone. It is correct that the gift is given only by grace, but the scriptures describe that in addition, works and the building of one's character qualifies one for the highest degree of salvation.

Faith that God wants to make us into better beings should motivate anyone to follow Christ's teachings and choose to overcome sin and align their will and lifestyle with God's commandments.

As stated by James, the Apostle and brother of Jesus, "faith without works is dead" and "by works was faith made perfect." These biblical references lead one to recognize the importance of works in building Christlike traits and becoming more like the Savior (see James 2:22, 26). To say that grace alone provides salvation to man ignores the teachings of the Savior and his apostles, where they describe necessary works—such as baptism, receiving the gift of the Holy Ghost, taking the sacrament, missionary work, discipleship, repenting, studying the scriptures, praying, testifying of Christ, fasting, caring for the sick and needy, mourning with those that mourn, and so on—as part of the process of becoming converted and attaining salvation *through* Christ. Mormon theology continues in this vein and teaches us to *learn* heaven and not simply earn heaven.

*"And other sheep I have, which are not of this fold:*
*them also I must bring, and they shall hear my voice;*
*and there shall be one fold, and one shepherd.*

—John 10:16

# 8

# More than One Book?

## The Book of Mormon

Red Flags and Misconceptions:

*Joseph Smith made up the Book of Mormon.*

*Revelation 22:18 says to not add to the Bible.*

*There is no archaeological evidence for the Book of Mormon.*

*The Book of Mormon is not mentioned in the Bible.*

*The Book of Mormon uses a French word.*

*The Book of Mormon says nothing of the three degrees of glory.*

Though several more "red flags" could have been addressed that are associated with the Book of Mormon, for the purpose of this book, I have limited our discussion to these stumbling blocks people run into during their first experiences reading or hearing about the Book of Mormon. The context of the Book of Mormon focuses on two things: 1) As a second witness to the Bible, it testifies of Christ, and 2) It tells of the history and downfall of two civilizations. The book is also one of the main reasons the LDS faith comes under scrutiny. Without delving too deep into the archaeological or scientific arguments, answering the above red flags and misconceptions should lead the honest religious investigator to the answers about the nature of this book. The book is a compilation of records, from many prophets' points of view, of the religious, political, and military history of two civilizations that existed on the American continent.

Gaining a testimony of the Book of Mormon is essential to any Latter-day Saint's conversion, much like the Ten Commandments were essential to the Israelite's. The Book of Mormon restores truths and further insight into doctrines taught in the Bible and acts as further support that God does reveal his word to his children. Being familiar with the Bible and having faith in Christ are important to the investigator of the LDS Church, because Christ is the central figure of all LDS religious worship. Because "Mormonism" is first and foremost a Christian faith founded on Christ's teachings, the Book of Mormon does not detract from the Bible, despite what some critics may presume.

For those who have found it to be confusing when Mormons talk about Jesus Christ being on the American continent, the Book of Mormon provides a picture of those "other sheep" that Christ refers to in his earthly sermons. The Book of Mormon teaches that after Christ's resurrection and after the time he spent in Judea with his original apostles, he came to visit the Book of Mormon people in his resurrected and immortal state. Many mainstream Christians find this claim unusual. But why? The Son of God has said he cares for all his children, not only those that we are familiar with in the Bible and are exclusive to the Eastern Hemisphere.

### A Second Witness of Christ

As a second witness of Christ, the Book of Mormon settles one of humanity's most significant spiritual questions: Why a belief in Christ? Why not Buddha, Krishna, or any number of other ancient gods? In a world becoming smaller and more interconnected and with cultural awareness and knowledge-sharing abounding like never before, Joseph Smith's revelation seems more relevant today as Christ-centered beliefs compete with Buddha or Krishna or other alternative spiritual beliefs. What spiritual message in all the world's libraries can compare with the dual claims of the Bible and the Book of Mormon? In his infinite wisdom, God provided a second witness to the ministry of his Son. Joseph Smith received a revelation describing one of the purposes of the Book of Mormon. In Doctrine and Covenants 20:11 (recorded in the year 1830), it states one of the many reasons for this second witness of Christ: "Proving to the world that the holy scriptures are true, and that God does inspire men and call them to his holy work in this age and generation, as well as in generations of old."

As stated before, with the increase of irreligion and secularism, and as more Westerners receive exposure to many other belief systems through globalization, the Bible's testament to the one true God is weakened because it stands alone as a witness of Christ in mainstream Christian circles, without the Book of Mormon. Thus to many practical or rational thinkers, any ancient god could hypothetically be just as real as the next if such a god is limited geographically and to a particular point in time. Judeo-Christian stories, principles, values, and commandments are already mocked and less accepted in society. For example, whether one agrees or disagrees with the politics of the issues, once-accepted areas of American life like praying in school and having the Ten Commandments on display in public places are now coming under condemnation for their religious nature. The emphasis and need for another witness of the God of Israel has profound significance even many generations after Joseph Smith.

### Revelation 22 Says, "Do Not Add to the Bible."

Before the Bible was canonized with its sixty-six books, John the Apostle wrote the book of Revelation during his exile on the Island of Patmos as a book in and of itself (Rev. 1:9-11). In a verse from the very end of Revelation, chapter 22 verses 18-19, lies one of the oldest complaints critics use to condemn the Book of Mormon. The verses exhort the reader to not add or take away from "this book" or "this prophecy." To know what "this book" is referring to, in Revelation 1:11 God tells John, "What thou seest, *write in a book* and send it to the seven churches which are in Asia." All the other Epistles written by the apostles are considered individual "books." Most critics view the verses in chapter 22 as saying, "Do not add to the *Bible*." But from the book of Revelation itself, it is clear that this verse is not talking about "a Bible" as we know it today, but rather the individual book of Revelation. While God did instruct John, "What thou seest, write in a book," he did not say, "What thou seest, write in the Bible" (as the Bible did not exist at that time). The book of Revelation stands alone in this context because the Bible had not been compiled at the time John wrote Revelation.

With the critic's logic, and also with Revelation 22:18-19, one could argue that anything in the Bible after Deuteronomy 4:2 is invalid by not recognizing the context in which the scripture is written. In this chapter Moses says: "Ye shall not add unto the word which I command you, neither shall ye diminish ought from it, that ye may keep the commands of the Lord your God which I command you."

Moses is not suggesting here that the last commands he has given Israel are all that God will ever again reveal to man. Rather, he is speaking to Israel in that respective time and place and telling them to obey the commands they have been given—to not change them, but to obey them as they were instructed. Not once does Moses suggest that he is the last prophet God will ever call or that God has revealed all that is necessary for man for all time. On what grounds, then, do critics claim that Mormonism cannot add to the Bible, or that the Bible is finished?

### Angels and Gold Plates?

When Joseph Smith first reported his visions, he attracted immediate criticism. Were visions not common amongst the peoples of the Bible? On what grounds did his peers judge so quickly? One reason may have been because Joseph Smith mentioned metal plates, but his peers and critics were not familiar with ancient writings on metal but rather with traditional ink and paper. In the Middle East, specifically Jerusalem predating Christ, the practice of scripture writing on metal did once exist. In the 1970s, silver scrolls that dated back 600 years before Christ were found in Jerusalem with the priestly prayer from the Old Testament book of Numbers engraved on them (Meyers, *Silver Scrolls' are oldest Old Testament scripture*; Holguin, *Science Unlocks Biblical Secrets*). The first Book of Mormon prophet, Lehi, left Jerusalem around 600 BC and is known to have continued this practice of recording in the Americas.

Again, this ancient scroll is dated back to the seventh century BC, precisely the same time and place where the Book of Mormon prophet Nephi obtained the plates of brass. It makes sense for Lehi and Nephi to have continued a practice they were familiar with, to engrave on metals that are easily shaped and which preserve better than papyrus. Beyond Jerusalem, metal plates have been discovered in Korea, Bulgaria, and ancient Persia.

### The Bible Does Not Mention the Book of Mormon.

For some, the mere fact that the Book of Mormon is not mentioned by name in the Bible is an immediate cause for doubt. Consider, however, that the Old Testament never mentions verbatim a New Testament or Jesus Christ. The words "Jesus Christ" are not found in the Old Testament at all. Rather than take the pessimistic approach to the Book of Mormon, one ought to read it and understand who its people are and the context in which they became the people of the Book of Mormon. The Book of Mormon story begins with the prophet Lehi and his family, who are commanded to flee Jerusalem. These events take place just before the Babylonians invade and carry the tribes of Israel into captivity. For his righteousness, Lehi's family, who are also a remnant of Israel, are guided to a land of promise in the Western Hemisphere.

The Book of Mormon does not replace the Bible, nor is it "the LDS Bible" or the "Mormon Bible." It has been and always will be, as the subtitle declares, *Another* Testament of Jesus Christ. This book threatens many because it is not the Bible, the book they have always been told is the "final word" of God. However, in LDS theology the Book of Mormon is referred to as the "stick of Joseph" spoken of in Ezekiel 37:16, 19, which describes a book, or "stick," coming from a people other than the tribe of Judah, who gave us the Old Testament, or the "stick of Judah." The Book of Mormon describes Lehi's family as from the tribe of Joseph.

Because people have the idea ingrained in their mind that the Bible is the only word of God, they tend to automatically reject anything else. From the previous chapters it is evident that the Bible is not the only word of God, nor did the biblical writers anticipate such a claim that their writings would be taken as the final written authority given to man until the second coming of Christ. The problem with accepting the Book of Mormon as a valid companion to the Bible is a human issue, one in which the mere idea of it does not fit preconceived notions or expectations or, in this case, man's interpretation that God provided mankind only one book. So when people say the Book of Mormon is not mentioned in the Bible, they are correct that it is not mentioned by that name. They might be surprised, however, to know that the Bible does talk about another book of scripture.

### A Book That Is Sealed: Biblical Reference to the Book of Mormon?

In Isaiah 29, it mentions a book that is sealed. In verse 10, it talks about spiritual blindness and God "covering" the prophets and seers, saying the "Lord hath poured out upon you the spirit of deep sleep and hath closed your eyes." This sounds reminiscent of an apostasy. What is this sealed book? In verse 11, it says the book is sealed, which may denote hiding or physically closing the record for a period of time. "Sealed" may also mean "unavailable to man until God opens the book, dependent upon righteousness." In 1 Corinthians 2:14, it says, "But the natural man receiveth not the things of the Spirit of God: for they are foolishness unto him: neither can he know them, because they are spiritually discerned." In Isaiah, it continues that the sealed book would be delivered to a man that is learned who would be asked to read it and would respond, "I cannot; for it is sealed." The book is then brought to another man who says, "I am not learned." However, God continues, saying in verse 14, "For the wisdom of their wise men shall perish, and the understanding of their prudent shall be hid." God says in verse 18, "In that day shall the deaf hear the words of the book, and the eyes of the blind shall see out of obscurity, and out of darkness." Verse 19: "The meek also shall increase their joy in the Lord, and the poor among men shall rejoice in the Holy One of Israel," who is Christ.

What book is Isaiah talking about? When is this great awakening going to take place? Why are the wise and prudent confounded while the meek and poor are rejoicing?

Joseph Smith, in need of financial assistance to publish the Book of Mormon, sought out a farmer named Martin Harris. Skeptical, Harris took excerpts of the Book of Mormon characters that Smith copied for him to Columbia University, where Harris met professor Charles Anthon. Professor Anthon, who prepared for Harris a certificate authenticating the characters, questioned how these characters came into being. Upon hearing that they came from the administering of angels, he tore up the certificate. Anthon proceeded to offer to translate the plates himself, until Martin replied that the book was sealed. Professor Anthon reportedly responded, "I cannot read a sealed book" (Hinckley, 74). Convinced of this "learned man's" verification, Martin returned to Joseph Smith and provided the funding by selling much of his estate.

From this story we find parallels to the verses in Isaiah. First, that a book would come forth that is sealed (Ether 3:22, 5:1; Moroni 10:2) and that it would be delivered to both the learned (Professor Anthon) and unlearned (the boy, Joseph Smith, who only had a third-grade education). Secondly, the meek and the poor, not the academic and professional peers of Joseph Smith's time, made up the membership of the LDS Church in its founding.

### The Book of Mormon Is in Archaic English, But It Uses the French Word "Adieu."

One characteristic that confuses new readers of the Book of Mormon is that it is written in Archaic English. Why? That was the biblical language in Joseph Smith's time, when the Book of Mormon was translated. The LDS Church still uses the King James Version Bible, so the Book of Mormon complements its language usage.

At the end of Jacob in the Book of Mormon, Jacob ends with the word "adieu." This has been used as a popular attack on the credibility of Joseph Smith's alleged creation. Critics point to the fact that French had not yet been invented in 500 BC, when Jacob recorded his words. Why would critics look at it as a problem with genuine Book of Mormon authorship? Obviously a person in the Book of Mormon held no connection with a country or language that did not exist. Critics fail to remember this book was translated for an intended audience—in this case Americans, who spoke English in 1830. Interestingly enough, Noah Webster's 1828 American Dictionary listed "adieu" as proper English. A complimentary factor to consider in the translation process is the use of the word "bruit" in the book of Jeremiah (Jeremiah 10:22). The word is French, yet Jeremiah wrote before 600 BC, and the translation in the King James Version carried this French word over, as did Joseph Smith. The translators used words found in the English of their time. This should not create a problem for Bible believers and honest seekers of truth.

### The Book of Mormon Does Not Mention the Three Degrees of Glory.

When the LDS Church says the Book of Mormon contains the fulness of the gospel, critics point out that the Book of Mormon describes two options for the afterlife: heaven or hell. However, the Book of Mormon also talks often of man being judged according to his works and describes rewards in heaven (Alma 41:11–15; see also Alma 3:26–27, 5:25). Many verses do describe or allude to salvation (speaking of the salvation that the saints seek, the celestial kingdom) or damnation that can be interpreted as halting one's eternal progression (gaining a glory of the moon or stars) or to the more extreme spiritual death, or outer darkness.

Why critics claim that Latter-day Saints contradict themselves, in this case, is understandable on the surface. The Book of Mormon does not contain all that Latter-day Saints believe. The Book of Mormon does contain the complete message of the Bible: faith in Christ, repentance, baptism, and enduring to the end of one's life. The Book of Mormon does not mention baptism for the dead, but it does mention baptism for salvation. It does not mention temple marriages, but it does mention the use of temples; it does not mention the LDS temple covenant, but it does mention covenant making.

To imagine that the Book of Mormon is a carbon copy of everything that makes up the LDS theology is misguided. In the New Testament it says certain mysteries "hath been hid from ages and from generations, but now is made manifest to his saints" (Colossians 1:26). In addition, the prophet Amos wrote, "Surely the Lord God will do nothing, but he revealeth his secret unto his servants the prophets" (Amos 3:7). The Book of Mormon is not a carbon copy of LDS theology, nor does it need to be; it is consistent too with the Old Testament not mentioning Jesus Christ by name, his apostles, and the details of their ministry. With only a written record, as the Book of Mormon is, it is difficult to expect that everything believed and practiced by Latter-day Saints, who also possess the spoken word today, would be wrapped up in this single volume of scripture. No one record of scripture can pass such a test. Scripture only builds or expounds upon previous scripture. Mormons believe the Book of Mormon provides greater and more detailed information than reading from the Bible alone. Further LDS doctrine as recorded by Joseph

Smith and other modern prophets even provide further revelation to the Book of Mormon. Just like the Bible does not give every detail of the Catholic tradition of Mass, the writings of the Book of Mormon and modern revelation have built up over the years the explanations, doctrines, and teachings within in the LDS Church.

### Conclusion

Critics can find many approaches to attack the Book of Mormon, whether through the use of the Bible, lack of archaeological evidence, word use, or arguing that the Book of Mormon is contradictory to the faith that it declares is truth. At first glance, such concerns appear legitimate, but a more honest approach says otherwise. The results show that the Bible and the Book of Mormon work together as one to strengthen their declaration of Christ as the Son of God.

Though one will not find everything that Latter-day Saints believe in the Book of Mormon, the core of the Christ's teachings are plainly manifest. The Book of Mormon speaks regularly on the plan of salvation, in which the prophets testify of life before the foundation of the world (premortal existence), the purpose of mortality, and the judgment of our character. The Book of Mormon also describes the justice and mercy of God, the laws of God, sin against the laws, covenant making, and the need for a Savior. The principles and teachings of faith, obedience, baptism, and being judged according to our works are repeated throughout the Book of Mormon, expressing the core teachings of the Gospel of Christ. If one looks at the bottom of each page in the Book of Mormon, there are many cross-references to the Bible, demonstrating that the books indeed complement one another.

*"And I saw another angel . . . having the everlasting gospel
to preach unto them that dwell on the earth, and to every nation,
and kindred, and tongue, and people."*

—Revelation 14:6

*"I asked the Personages who stood above. . .which of all the sects was right. . .and which I should join. I was answered that I must join none of them, for they were all wrong; and the Personage who addressed me said that all their creeds were an abomination."*

—Joseph Smith—History 1:18-19

# 9

# Many Reforms, One Restoration

## Joseph Smith and the Primitive Church

### Red Flags and Misconceptions:

*Mormons are not part of historic Christianity.*
*Mormonism is a cult.*

In the spring of 1820, after reading James chapter 1 verse 5—which states, "If any of you lack wisdom, let him ask of God"—fourteen-year-old Joseph Smith accepted this challenge, and as a result he received a visitation from the divine. Both Christ and the Father appeared and answered Smith's simple question of which church to join. As bold as Smith's First Vision appears, it raises the question: Why would God not reveal himself again in our day as he did throughout the Bible? Smith's legacy will forever be attached to the bold statements from his First Vision, assertions that critics view negatively. All presumptions aside from what one knows—or thinks they know—about Mormonism, such a bold declaration seeks to invoke a positive feeling of change in the knowledge that God has spoken and is asking man to question the traditions they have inherited. It is not a new thing for the God of the Bible to ask man to have an inner reflection and to consider his station or the traditions that he possesses.

For critics, this statement offends the belief systems of many Christians whose traditions were in place long before Joseph Smith's revelation. Among the larger Protestant sects of Smith's day, Mormonism appeared out of the ordinary because Protestants were not familiar with direct heavenly visitations and felt God no longer spoke to man because the heavens were closed. Thus many postulated that the Bible was the only source of God's word and that Smith was adding to the Bible.

The 2012 race for the Republican nomination for President of the United States once again brought Mormonism under the microscope. Dr. Robert Jeffress, a Dallas pastor who came out in support of Texas Governor Rick Perry, made the statement that Mormonism is widely accepted as a "theological cult" amongst his peer mainstream Christians and that "they [Mormons] have never been considered part of historical Christianity" (*Mediate, Frances Martel*). This chapter will challenge the long-standing divide between Mormons and mainstream Christians, while showing that Joseph Smith, through God, sought only to reinstitute the doctrines of the primitive Gospel.

Table 9.1 shows that the Bible provides evidence of a kingdom to be reestablished in the last days. Ancient prophets foretold of a time when the God of Israel and his kingdom would fill the earth and stand forever. Because of the Great Apostasy, the fulness of the gospel and its keys of authority were not available for man to commence in building this kingdom. Recall in Revelation 13 where Satan "overcame the saints." In Revelation 14, it describes a time when an angel shall come forth from heaven to bring the gospel to all the earth. After 1500 years since the last apostles and direct communication with God, many Protestant reformers with their newfound access to the written word sought to hasten the Millennium and Second Coming of Christ.

### In Search of First-Century Christianity

In the centuries prior to Joseph Smith's encounter with the divine in the Sacred Grove, "Countless American Christians . . . rushed to

**Table 9.1**

**Biblical References to a Post–New Testament Restoration**

| | |
|---|---|
| Isaiah 2:2 | And it shall come to pass in the last days, that the mountain of the Lord's house shall be established in the top of the mountains, and shall be exalted above the hills; and all nations shall flow unto it. |
| Isaiah 29:14 | Therefore, behold, I will proceed to do a marvelous work among this people, even a marvelous work and a wonder: for the wisdom of their wise men shall perish, and the understanding of their prudent men shall be hid. |
| Daniel 2:44 (Also see Jeremiah 31:31) | And in the days of these kings shall the God of heaven set up a kingdom, which shall never be destroyed: and the kingdom shall not be left to other people, but it shall break in pieces and consume all these kingdoms, and it shall stand for ever. |
| Acts 3:21 | Whom the heavens must receive until the times of restitution of all things. |
| Romans 11:25, 28 | Blindness in part is happened to Israel, until the fullness of the Gentiles be come in. As concerning the gospel, they (Israel) are enemies for your sakes; but as touching the election, they are beloved for their fathers' sakes. |
| Ephesians 1:10 | In the dispensation of the fullness of times he might gather together in one all things in Christ. |
| Revelations 14:6 | And I saw another angel fly in the midst of heaven, having the everlasting gospel to preach unto them that dwell on the earth, and to every nation, and kindred, and tongue, and people. |

discover the pattern of the primitive church, to rebuild that church in the new American nation, and thereby to hasten the millennial age." (Allen, *Discovering Our Roots: The Ancestry of Churches of Christ*, 92). Roger Williams, cofounder of the province of Rhode Island and the first Baptist Church in America, was not convinced that the true church with all the proper ordinances was on the earth at that time. He said, "There is no regularly constituted church of Christ on earth, nor any person qualified to administer any church ordinances; nor can there be until new apostles are sent by the Great Head of the Church for whose coming I am seeking" (Bryan, *Picturesque America, or the Land We Live* In, 502). William's admission raises an important question: Since the time of Christ and his apostles, whom has God ordained to administer in his church like the prophets of old? As learned men ordained themselves to the ministry with Bible in hand (recall the Pharisees and Sadducees who possessed the Old Testament writings without a prophet to interpret and preside over the offices of their faith), Roger Williams noticed key biblical elements missing amongst his Christian contemporaries.

Many biblical prophets in both the Old and New Testaments foretold of a time when the gospel in its fulness would be restored, as previously stated. From previous chapters, it can be concluded that an apostasy occurred after the death of Christ's apostles, and post–New Testament traditions entered in. Table 9.1, on the previous page, provides several examples throughout scripture that prophesy of the rebuilding of God's kingdom in the last days. While each dispensation is preceded with the calling of a prophet, Joseph Smith was called by God the Father to bring forth this restoration in the last days.

## Church Priesthood and Structure Restored

The cycle of apostasy and restoration is a common theme in the biblical pattern; so too is the restoration and loss of the priesthood. Authority to hold the priesthood is historically passed on from Christ or his chosen vessels. This priesthood exists simultaneously with each restoration and ceases to exist with each apostasy. In modern times, Joseph Smith recorded his calling and having been bestowed with this priesthood power by those who last held the keys: John the Baptist, Elijah, Peter, James, and John. This power is expressed in the LDS

Church to heal the sick, bless newborns, baptize, and call members to church offices (deacons, teachers, priests, and elders). Another aspect of the priesthood unique to LDS theology is the power to seal, bind, or loosen eternal covenants such as marriage (Matthew 16:19).

As previously stated, apostles and prophets make up the foundation of Church leadership, as taught in Ephesians 2:20. However, there is another important component of this leadership structure within each dispensation of Christ's church, and it was also restored by Joseph Smith. This is the "Quorum of the Seventy," a group of men called to assist the apostles and prophets. Evidence of this group of seventy is mentioned as early as Exodus (Exodus 24:1—"And he said unto Moses, Come up unto the Lord . . . and seventy of the elders of Israel; and worship ye afar off."), in the time of the later prophets in the Old Testament (Ezekiel 8:11—"And there stood before them seventy men of the ancients of the house of Israel."), and the Gospel according to Luke (Luke 10:1—"After these things the Lord appointed other seventy also."). They exist today in the restored Church. If a church were being restored, it would be similar in features to its primitive predecessor. Much like the seventy elders in the time of Moses, Ezekiel, and Christ, Joseph Smith restored this office in modern times to assist in building the kingdom.

In these two examples, Joseph Smith's revelations and the practices in LDS theology harken back to the Bible. First, the binding power to seal a marriage for eternity contrasts with the traditional marriage oath that states "till death do us part." Second, the ancient offices found in the Bible were restored and are not found amongst other denominations.

### Called from His Humble Station

Unlike many of the clergy in colonial America, who trained in formal seminaries, Joseph Smith's call as prophet began at age fourteen when he had less than a third-grade education. Joseph Smith did not seek to bring about a restoration from his own work, study, and philosophy like his peer reformers and his predecessors. A reading from James 1:5 of the New Testament began the journey for Joseph Smith. Through the power of the Holy Ghost, Joseph Smith revealed things that had been lost to the earth for nearly two thousand years. The Restoration of the primitive church in modern times came through answers dictated by God as responses to questions Smith became concerned with in his own study of the Bible and in listening to the preachers in his community. The process of restoration came through months and years of revelation and learning, similar to other prophets' tutoring (such as Moses's on Mt. Horeb, or Samuel's in the Old Testament). Joseph Smith's prophetic calling to restore gospel truths to man and rebuild God's kingdom on earth was accomplished in a humble manner much like the birth of the Savior: not widely heralded or known, and given "precept upon precept; line upon line" (Isaiah 28:10).

Consider how some key characteristics of mainstream Christianity differ from the restoration of truth that Smith brought forth. First, mainstream Christianity has never claimed direct contact with Deity; they support the idea of a closed canon, and they have doctrines which are not definitively characteristic of the New Testament. Joseph Smith reported direct contact with God the Father and his Son, much like Moses who spoke with God face to face (Deuteronomy 34:10). LDS belief supports further revelation through prophets, and its traditions seek to restore and are parallel with the New Testament and other first- and second-century writings that are extra-biblical.

As highlighted in some of the previous chapters, many of the doctrines revealed to Joseph Smith echo the writings of early Christians writers Justin Martyr, Origen, Tertullian, and others. Each of these Christian writers adds a touch of significance to the doctrinal matters that Joseph Smith restored. These early Christian writings were not available in America until the late nineteenth century; Joseph Smith was martyred in 1844. Recall some examples of what these writers helped to clarify: the nature of God the Father and the Savior, degrees of reward in the resurrection, and failed leadership in the early church after the apostles.

These points set Joseph Smith apart from the typical Christian reformers who relied upon the Bible and their formal education, which guided these individuals to create a variety of Christian traditions they believed to be consistent with the Bible. Smith, however, as in the example of Moses, who was slow of speech, lacked formal training for his calling, which is congruent with God's pattern of calling prophets who do not appear by man's standards to be qualified to lead God's work. In relation to this, there is a Christian saying that says, "God doesn't call the qualified, he qualifies the called."

### Can Mormonism Really Be Defined as a Cult?

As defined in chapter 1, a cult is a religious group devoted to a particular character. Another definition simply states that cults have practices that are considered sinister or strange. What most critics or other Christians do not realize when they call Mormons a "cult" is how similar LDS beliefs are to both mainstream Christianity and early Christianity. Mormons accept:

- The Godhead: Father, Son, and the Holy Spirit (biblical)
- The laying on of hands by God's authority
- The Old and New Testaments, as well as additional scripture
- Baptism as a symbol of our commitment to obey the Lord and to be cleansed of our sins, an opportunity given to a person who can choose to be baptized—age 8 and up, not infants, in LDS doctrine
- Christmas
- Easter and the death and resurrection of our Lord and Savior Jesus Christ
- Sabbath observance (and all of the Ten Commandments)
- Prophets, apostles, bishops, deacons, priest, seventies, elders, and other biblical offices
- Grace, works, faith, obedience, repentance, and fellowship
- Feeding the hungry, clothing the naked, sheltering the homeless, caring for the elderly and sick, and other Christlike service

In addition to what Mormons have in common with mainstream Christians, the biblical text further backs LDS doctrines not accepted by the other traditions. Cited throughout this book are scriptures that show biblical evidence for the following uniquely LDS doctrines:

- Salvation/baptism for the dead
- Premortal existence
- Plural marriage in its correct understanding
- Glories of heaven and being judged according to our works
- Unpaid clergy and their freedom to marry
- Man's potential to become like God and Christ

- The need for living apostles and prophets
- Recognition of the biblical pattern of apostasy and restoration
- Recognition that a single faith can exist today, directed by God as it was throughout the Bible

When mainstream Christianity recognizes that there are common biblical beliefs between themselves and Mormons, more religious understanding and strength of unity, or being one in Christ, may be realized (John 17:21).

## Conclusion

The Protestant Reformation began a mere 300 years before Joseph Smith and the Restoration, or what is known to the world as "Mormonism." Smith did not intend to create a religion or theology called "Mormonism"; he merely sought to understand the truth behind the various sects of his day and which among them was established by God. In comparison, the reform movements occurring at the same time as Smith's experience sought to reestablish primitive Christianity. The reform movements inspired the formation of many sects independent of the once-dominant Catholic (and later, Anglican) churches, in a time period historians have designated the "Great Awakening." To constrain the discovery of ancient truths to a specific time period, with a set beginning and end, limits the power of God to continue to shed light on biblical truths. While "historic Christians," as defined by Pastor Jeffress and other critics, have been eager to dismiss Smith and LDS theology, they have done so without exploring the biblical basis of such doctrines discussed in this book. The Restoration was not meant to prove other churches wrong any more or less than were the reformers who broke away from the Catholic and Anglican systems. Man was simply becoming aware of truths hidden plainly before them and unlocking them as access to the written word became more available. To an extent, man without God has limitations. This book has shown that God often calls prophets to reveal hidden truths, which almost always oppose the ideas or doctrines that man postulates from his own mind or interpretation.

In light of the early American religious traditions, "Mormonism" appeared unchristian because Mormons rejected the creeds and councils fashioned at Nicaea and many other seemingly post–New Testament traditions that crept in over the centuries. As a result of this rejection, is it fair to label Mormonism as a cult? Or is it because of the late arrival of Mormonism on the scene in religious history that many do not lend the faith very much credit? How do the teachings of the Bible match up with LDS theology or doctrine?

In light of the Restoration, the Bible speaks of a kingdom that would be built in the last days and that would stand forever and fill the earth. God told the prophet Isaiah that this "marvelous work" would proceed among men and that "the wisdom of their wise men shall perish" (Isaiah 29:14). Just as Jesus confounded the teachings of the respected religious authorities of his day, an unlearned farm boy in 1820s upstate New York brought forth revelation and clarification of lost or neglected biblical truths that challenged the dogmas of mainstream Christian thought. Unique characteristics to this Restoration in comparison to other reform efforts include direct, face-to-face contact with Deity; new scripture; and doctrines that support written history of the Old and New Testaments as well as first- and second-century Christian documents. This Restoration fulfilled not only the promise to Isaiah, but also fulfilled the New Testament, which foretells of the "fulness of times" and a time when all would be gathered together "in one" (Ephesians 1:10). The restored gospel was prophesied to spread among all peoples and nations as a mechanism by which all would be gathered together. "The Standard of Truth has been erected; no unhallowed hand can stop the work from progressing. . . . The truth of God will go forth boldly, nobly, and independent, till it has penetrated every continent . . . and sounded in every ear, till the purposes of God shall be accomplished, and the Great Jehovah shall say the work is done" (History of the Church, 4:540).

LDS theology parallels many well-known beliefs held in common with mainstream Christianity while rejecting doctrines adopted after the death of Christ's original apostles. The Mormon teachings that come under the most scrutiny or that are labeled unique, peculiar, or cult-like, and those that create stigmas against the the LDS Church are surprisingly rooted in the Bible. Mormonism pushes the conversation of religious understanding forward, coupled with the reestablishment of revelation to man through modern prophets, apostles, and scripture. These elements that are uniquely LDS manifest that God is interested in the affairs of mankind with his involvement in the prophesied last days to build his kingdom.

*"The Lord hath chosen thee to be a peculiar people unto himself."*

—Deuteronomy 14:2

# 10

# Other Misunderstandings

## Answered with the Bible

Red Flags and Misconceptions:

*Jesus drank wine, so why can't we?*

*Don't force your beliefs on me.*

*The Bible says God doesn't dwell in buildings, so why go to church?*

*Mormon chapels looks like a courtroom, and the services are boring.*

*Why do Mormons baptize their dead?*

*Joseph smith boasted to be greater than Christ.*

*Brigham Young said, "There is no salvation without belief in Joseph Smith."*

The previous chapters showed how LDS doctrine parallels primitive Christianity. Some Mormon beliefs differ from mainstream Christianity, and these differences have led to mistrust and misunderstanding and have separated our fellow Bible-believing friends from the truths of the Restoration. Below is a brief review of the negative commentary this book has already covered that cause many to turn away from the LDS faith:

- Former practice of plural marriage
- That the LDS Church does not embrace the "Bible only," but rather looks to modern prophets and apostles to supplement the ancient and inspired records.

- Disregard for the Trinity as proposed in the fourth-century Creeds
- That good works save, not Christ
- Mormons preach "another gospel"
- Mormons "will get their own planet"

This chapter will discuss other reasons why the LDS faith is misunderstood. They include LDS views on alcohol; young missionaries sent out to "force religion" on others; and issues on worship, temples, and other symbolism.

### Jesus, Wine, and the Word of Wisdom

Joseph Smith received a revelation (recorded in Doctrine and Covenants 89) for the Saints to refrain from certain substances—including tobacco, alcohol, and "hot drinks" (tea and coffee)—as a common health code known as the Word of Wisdom. Considering common incidents today in which many people drink to a dangerous level, it is no wonder that a faith claiming to be a restoration of the early Church commanded its faithful members to avoid dangerous habits.

Although Latter-day Saints are often seen as peculiar for not drinking alcohol, God has always condemned drunkenness. To the Galatians, Paul writes, speaking of this topic, "That they which do such things shall not inherit the kingdom of God" (Galatians 5:21). One may consider this language harsh or take it further and consider themselves beyond salvation. However, there is a difference between sinning once and living a lifestyle without going through the repentance process. In my humble opinion, repentance is an option for someone who has lived years in drunkenness but who seeks Christ and redemption; Paul's words to the Galatians are for those who know of their wrongdoing and who reject the opportunity to change while given the chance.

Further, God asks nothing less of his Saints than to "avoid the appearance of evil" (1 Thessalonians 5:22). God knows the nature of the world, the behavior of man in relation to the drink, and that alcohol is a mind-altering drug. For some, alcohol may be a substance enjoyed in moderation. But for every single act of moderation there is the opportunity to lead others into a lifetime of addiction.

Abstinence from drinking can help to avoid a lifetime of addiction, abuse, societal ills, and even fatality. By avoiding the appearance of evil and abstaining from this harmful substance, one can draw closer to God as they follow his commandments. Alcohol is an addictive, mind-altering substance that causes more problems than it does good. The Word of Wisdom protects everyone—even the weakest among us; while not everyone has a problem with drunkenness, there are many who struggle with addiction and allow alcohol to affect their health and relationships.

How does the Bible reader reconcile these teachings of avoiding drunkenness and the appearance of evil with the fact that Jesus provided wine at a wedding? The New Testament says Jesus provided what the Bible calls "wine" for a wedding—surely not a scene comparable to taking down several shots at the local bar with the gang on a Friday night to become completely intoxicated for the sake of intoxication. Additionally, wine was a common drink in Christ's time because water was scarce or unclean. But was all wine fermented? LDS Apostle Bruce R. McConkie stated that the wine in the New Testament was the "fruit of the vine (Matthew 26:29), a light, sweet wine (normally unfermented); eaten with bread, it was one of the staple foods of the day" (Doctrinal New Testament Commentary, 1:136).

Modernly, drinking is used as an escape more often than not, to forget one's trials or to delay dealing with them. Drunkenness is embraced as a fad or seen as a right of passage for college-aged and even high school–aged kids. God provides hardship and challenges in life not so we can drink them away, but so we can better our condition and mature our character by paying attention to the lessons we are meant to learn.

### Eighteen-Year-Old Missionaries?

For some, the idea of an eighteen-year-old knocking on the door of an elderly person, for example, who has potentially studied the world's faith, feels insulting. People may also feel pressured by the young missionaries to be baptized, or feel inconvenienced when an unwelcome stranger knocks on their door. Admittedly, many get rubbed the wrong way by these young men and women, and many fail to understand their intent. Depending on one's perspective, the

Mormon missionary program can seem intimidating and may be seen as missionaries forcing their religion on others. Although many people are not interested, there are also many who *are* searching for answers about religion and who welcome the missionaries.

A key element in the primitive Christian Church was the traveling missionary work of the apostles. In order to spread the message of the gospel, God commissions and sends out missionaries to teach and convert. In Matthew 24:15, Jesus says, "This gospel of the kingdom shall be preached in all the world for a witness unto all nations; and then shall the end come." The biblical premise behind the missionary program is to mold disciples of Christ to be "fishers of men" (Matthew 4:19). Further, Jesus says, "Go ye therefore, and teach all nations, baptizing them in the name of the Father, and of the Son, and of the Holy Ghost" (Matthew 28:19).

Just as in the New Testament times, the LDS Church calls missionaries to spread the message of the Restoration to the entire world. As a "right of passage," so to speak, the LDS Church encourages all worthy male members to prepare in advance to serve a two-year, full-time mission when they reach the age of eighteen or nineteen, and women may choose to serve at the age of nineteen for eighteen months. This period provides a time for young people to better educate themselves on the gospel, and the perception the world has of their religion, and to ultimately be instruments in God's hand by gathering others who are searching for the gospel. While many eighteen-year-olds at this stage in life are focused on themselves, missionaries selflessly sacrifice their time to focus on God and service to mankind. As emissaries of Christ, most missionaries at this age have had years of education and are well equipped to introduce most truth seekers to the knowledge of the Restoration.

## Places of Worship

There are some who justify their spirituality by saying that "God does not dwell in temples" or buildings (Acts 17:24); these people would rather seek God in mountain streams or the sunset. Pastor Lillian Daniel of *Stillspeaking Daily Devotionals* uses humor to soften this debate as she responds to this line of thinking, "Like people who go to church don't see God in the sunset! Like we are these monastic little hermits who never leave the church building. How lucky we are to have these geniuses inform us that God is in nature. As if we don't hear that in the psalms, the creation stories and throughout our deep tradition" (Daniel, *Spiritual But Not Religious? Please Stop Boring Me!*).

There are those who feel they are robbed of a personal relationship with God by attending a church building. They often recite the words of Paul, who says God does not dwell in buildings or things made by men's hands. In the proper context, Paul was preaching to the Grecians in Athens at Mars Hill, to a superstitious group worshipping "the UNKNOWN GOD," whom Paul rebuked by saying that "we ought not to think the Godhead is like unto gold, or silver, or stone, or graven by art and by man's device" (Acts 17:22–29). Paul's comments about God not dwelling in temples (and things made with men's hands) are incorrectly used to denounce Christians who worship in church buildings. Paul's preaching was meant to focus worship away from physical objects or idols made of gold, silver, and stone, and to turn hearts and minds toward choosing the Christian lifestyle.

Buildings are convenient, provide a comfortable physical setting away from the weather, and provide the fellowship for a community of believers. They also provide the world with a visual of a people united as one. While appreciating nature is a way to honor God, he has asked that we assemble ourselves together (Hebrews 10:24–25) to discuss doctrines and come together in an environment of learning.

For more on Christian worship, C. S. Lewis described church attendance, daily prayer, and scripture reading as necessities for a Christian life. His premise was based on human nature and mood changes. After one accepts Christianity they must expose themselves to its doctrines to be "continually reminded of what we believe. Neither this belief nor any other will automatically remain alive in the mind. It must be fed" (Lewis, 141).

### Styles of Worship, Music, and Symbolism

When members of the Church bring investigators to Sunday worship, because of the difference of LDS services and what others are used to, explaining what to expect might go a long way. Investigators of religion may make their choice of church service by the style of worship, the architecture, the music, or whatever captures their interest or expectations. Worship in LDS meetinghouses is a different experience from many contemporary Christian services. In market Christianity, churches mail out brochures or post on online forums suggesting that their style of worship is the cure for a dead and boring church service. Such an advertisement seems to market Christianity in such a way that implies that one's current church service and devotion to God are incomplete without a form of contemporary entertainment during worship.

LDS worship focuses on teaching doctrine from the scriptures while some hymns or musical numbers add to the spirit. Those ranging from the young to the old share messages or sermons and are chosen from among the congregation by local leadership. Prayer and reverent music complement LDS worship, in contrast to having musical entertainment be the dominant aspect, as you might seen in many contemporary services. Recall the scene of Jesus washing the feet of his disciples or the Last Supper. Imagine what the scene would have looked like: quiet and reverent as they met and talked for the last time. However, during the course of their meeting before they left for the Mount of Olives, they "had sung an hymn" (Matthew 26:30).

The focus of the New Testament preached the word of God, called men to repentance, and exhorted obedience, all to build the kingdom and to develop individual righteousness. The focus during LDS worship is on the Last Supper, the suffering in Gethsemane, and the atoning sacrifice of Jesus on the cross, in addition to hymns or choirs during the main hour of service, known as sacrament meeting. It is a time of personal reflection that Latter-day Saints are blessed with each Sunday to remember the covenants they made with Christ at baptism. Leviticus 19:30 states, "Ye shall keep my sabbaths, and reverence my sanctuary."

In addition to the lack of a band and contemporary music, one might wonder why LDS chapels do not display a cross or other signs associated with Christian worship. Some might state that without these symbols, LDS chapels look like courtrooms and do not reflect what one would expect to see in a Christian church. There is no mention of the cross being displayed or used in New Testament–era worship, and the cross itself was the tool of choice for putting criminals to death in the Roman empire. Admittedly, LDS chapels do lack the display of this historic symbol. But that a symbol is old and presumably characteristic of primitive Christianity does not by default make

Mormons less Christian for choosing not to display it.

Though crosses are not displayed, Mormons still celebrate the resurrected Christ; and though he died, he died so man can live again. To speak to this argument, all LDS chapels display pictures of the Savior's life, death, and resurrection, which are the focus of LDS worship. These are a reminder of Christ's ministry and the Atonement, and allow one to worship with simple reminders of his sacrifice and of the purpose of attending church to renew covenants. Other pictures of scriptural figures are also included, as a reminder of those whose Christian lives are worth emulating. In contrast, anyone who has been in a Catholic church or relates the European style and décor with Christianity may be confused with the LDS chapel's simplicity. The plainness of these chapels, devoid of extravagance, does not distract from focusing on the spirit of the message.

### What about Temples and Salvation for the Dead?

Next to the worship of God himself, worship in the temple acted as the channel to reach to God for the ancient Israelites. The temple was the house of the Lord. In the Holy of Holies, the Ten Commandments were preserved in the ark of the covenant. In this way, the temple represented a place to make and keep covenants. Outside of the temple, a large basin on the backs of twelve oxen, which represented the twelve tribes of Israel, was used for ritual washings. As a sign of their covenant with and love of the Lord, Israelites offered the first of their flocks, symbolic of the coming Savior to be sacrificed for the sins of mankind. The temples and earlier altars used in Adam's or Abraham's time were fundamental to the worship of the God of Abraham, Isaac, and Jacob.

In one of the most dramatic scenes of Christ's life (Matthew 21:12–13), in reaction to his frustration that the moneychangers transformed the temple, a house of prayer, into a "den of thieves," Christ cast them out. Often in the New Testament, after Christ's life and ministry, the apostles mention gathering together in the temple (Acts 2:46, 3:1–2). Few details are recorded in the New Testament about the nature of their temple worship, but for what purposes would the Saints gather together in a temple? The New Testament says they prayed. Like ancient Israel, presumably they discussed the new covenant and used the temple as a means to learn and receive enlightenment regarding the Christian faith and what God expected of his disciples.

The Latter-day Saints claim to be a restoration of early Christianity, and therefore a restoration of the temple came about. Latter-day Saints build and use temples for a few reasons: marriage, covenant making, spiritual education, praying, and baptism for the dead. Of these temple practices, baptism for the dead receives the most inquiry and misunderstanding.

In LDS temples, Mormons perform baptism on behalf of the dead. Understanding the need for salvation of those who have died without receiving the opportunity to enter into the covenant of baptism is important for one to understand the need for this proxy ordinance. What happens to those who die without ever knowing Jesus Christ? This very question troubled the young Joseph Smith after his oldest brother, Alvin, passed away before being baptized. What then of the millions or even billions who have not received or never will receive baptism in this life? In the winter of 1836, the Lord gave Joseph Smith an answer to his concern:

> All who have died without a knowledge of this gospel, who would have received it if they had been permitted to tarry, shall be heirs of the celestial kingdom of God; Also all that shall die henceforth without a knowledge of it, who would have received it with all their hearts, shall be heirs of that kingdom; For I, the Lord, will judge all men according to their works, according to the desire of their hearts. (Doctrine and Covenants 137:7–9)

Those who died without receiving this ordinance and accepting or having heard the gospel of Christ would be given a chance. Learning this relieved Joseph Smith's concern, because a preacher told him that his brother would be damned to hell for not having received baptism. In Doctrine and Covenants 127, the Lord reveals his desire for Joseph Smith and the Saints to perform baptism for those who died without receiving this saving ordinance.

To again connect a doctrine that appears uniquely LDS to the Bible, in 1 Corinthians 15:29, Paul asks, "Else what shall they do which are baptized for the dead, if the dead rise not at all? Why are they then baptized for the dead?" Further, in the Gospel of Matthew (12:31–32) Christ talks of forgiveness being granted or restricted not in this life only, but *in the life to come.*

> Wherefore I say unto you, All manner of sin and blasphemy shall be forgiven unto men: but the blasphemy against the Holy Ghost shall not be forgiven unto men. And whosoever speaketh a word against the Son of man, it shall be forgiven him: but whosoever speaketh against the Holy Ghost, it shall not be forgiven him, neither in this world, neither in the world to come. (Matthew 12:31–32)

These verses counter the traditional thinking that one simply passes through this life having one chance to receive Christ, and therefore salvation. The description in verse 32 foreshadows the opportunity for forgiveness to be accepted or rejected not only in this life, but in the world to come. One of the reasons Mormons research family genealogy is to baptize those in their family who did not receive baptism while they were living. It is believed that those spirits that have passed on into spirit prison are granted an opportunity to hear Christ's gospel. Ultimately it is up to the individuals to accept Christ in this life and in the spirit world. Recall in 1 Peter 4, Christ preaching to the spirits in prison. Baptizing our dead turns our hearts and service toward those who came before us, as this earthly ordinance is extended to them.

Christ began his ministry reading from the book of Esaias (or Isaiah, the Old Testament prophet, Isaiah 61:1–2), as recorded in Luke 4:18. Christ describes his ministry as delivering the captives, or those in a spiritual prison. Recall from earlier discussion the LDS concepts of spirit paradise and spirit prison—the latter called "prison" because its inhabitants have not accepted Christ. In this life, there are some Christians who speak of people who have not accepted Christ as being in a sort of prison. But in context, Christ is referring to those who have died without having been reborn through baptism. Doing baptisms for the dead allows for those who did not have the opportunity on earth to be baptized and enter into the covenant with Christ. In the Book of Mormon, 2 Nephi 9:23 says, "And he commandeth all men that they must repent, and be baptized in his name, having perfect faith in the Holy One of Israel, or they cannot be saved in the kingdom of God." Also, in John 3:5 Christ tells Nicodemus, "Except a man be born of water and of the Spirit, he cannot enter into the kingdom of God."

In the book of Malachi, an interesting statement connects the human family, living and deceased. Malachi records, "Behold,

I will send you Elijah the prophet before the coming of the great and dreadful day of the Lord: And he shall turn the heart of the fathers to the children, and the heart of the children to their fathers, lest I come and smite the earth with a curse" (Malachi 4:5–6). This verse explicitly refers to a future time, just before the Lord returns. During this time, the hearts of both the living and deceased are turned toward one another. An expression or symbol of this is a loved one performing the saving temple work for their deceased loved ones.

### Attacks That Originate from Other LDS Writings and Journals

Did Joseph Smith boast to have accomplished a greater work than Jesus Christ and his apostles? This attack on LDS theology comes from a volume of books known as the *History of the Church*, volume 6, in which Smith says, "I have more to boast of than any man. . . . I am the only man that has been able to keep a whole church together. . . . Neither Paul, John, Peter, nor Jesus ever did it" (*History of the Church* 6, 408). From these same arguments, critics claim Latter-day Saints are ignorant of their own history. Considering all the effort Smith gave and the things he suffered for what he knew to be the work of Christ, this is simply a human flaw. It is not—nor will it ever be—Church policy to teach that Smith is somehow greater than Jesus Christ. The only thing that can be said is that Smith is correct in that he had done a greater work, in sheer numbers, but a work that Christ himself had commissioned of Smith. In John 14:12, Christ himself says, "He that believeth on me, the works that I do shall he do also; and greater works than these shall he do; because I go unto my Father." Since Christ is all-knowing, it is no surprise for him to admit that at some point a greater work would be accomplished. Today, the LDS Church is present on most continents, LDS literature is printed in most of the world's languages, and—by the sheer quantity of members of the restored Church—the *work* Joseph Smith accomplished proved to be "greater," as Jesus said. Prior to Smith's recorded boast, he said:

> As Paul boasted, I have suffered more than Paul did. I should be like a fish out of water, if I were out of persecutions. . . . I glory in persecution. I am not nearly so humble as if I were

> not persecuted. . . . If they want a beardless boy to whip all the world, I will get on the top of a mountain and crow like a rooster; I shall always beat them. When facts are proved, truth and innocence will prevail at last. My enemies are no philosophers: they think . . . they will keep me down—but for the fools, I will hold on and fly over them. (*History of the Church*, vol. 6, 408. https://byustudies.byu.edu/hc/hcpgs/hc.aspx?HC=/hc/6/1.html&A=408)

Ultimately, this recorded volume amounts to public statement, and it sounds as language unbecoming of a prophet. In comparison, the prophet Moses, in a heated moment, took upon himself to smite the rock with his rod and bring forth water to the stubborn Israelites rather than follow God who said, "Speak ye unto the rock before their eyes." For this boast or disobedient act, the Lord forbade Moses to enter into the promised land (Numbers 20:8-12). What must not be assumed is that prophets are somehow protected from making the same mistakes as anyone else.

Another statement by former LDS prophet Brigham Young feels unbecoming of a Christian leader. To discredit Mormonism, many critics refer to a comment that Young made saying, "There is no salvation without belief in Joseph Smith" to discredit Mormonism. This statement, taken out of context, does appear to lend credence to the argument that Mormons teach that there is no salvation without faith in Joseph Smith. From this criticism, people often confuse Mormon beliefs as worshipping Joseph Smith. What Young did say, however, is that "There is no salvation without belief in Joseph Smith *as a prophet of God*" (Journal of Discourses 4:54, italics added).

Interestingly, the Bible also provides evidence to support the idea that prophets in their own day are called of God and therefore essential to one's salvation as their words are truly God's own words. In John 13:20 it reads, "Verily, verily, I say unto you, He that receiveth whomsoever I send receiveth me; and he that receiveth me receiveth him that sent me." About being received into heaven by a prophet, Matthew 19:27–28 states that the apostles will judge the twelve tribes of Israel. This is repeated again in Luke 22:29–30 and Revelation 20:4. If one must accept the words of the apostles to find salvation in Christ, then surely the same principle applies if other prophets and apostles are called. Recall that Brigham Young emphasized belief in Smith as a *prophet*. Mormons affirm that Smith was a prophet, but he was also human, and like his predecessors (other prophets throughout the Bible), he made mistakes and received chastisement and teachings from God.

## Conclusion

Much of this chapter touched on cultural stigmas associated with the LDS Church and its leadership. Mormonism differs from other Christian denominations in some of its symbolism or worship services, but it also maintains similarities. Putting questioned topics in their proper context have shown, with support from ancient scripture, that LDS practice is very much in step with the Old and New Testaments.

When speaking to fellow Christians of other denominations, it helps to build on what they already understand. For example, many people understand that Mormons use water instead of wine in sacrament meeting and that a cross is not displayed in LDS chapels. When speaking to critics, being aware of arguments supposedly supported by the New Testament to try and show contradictions—like when Paul said God "dwelleth not in temples" or "neither is worshipped with men's hands"—it is important to be ready with an intelligent answer. Critics accuse Mormons of secrecy in their temples when the answer is simply that these things are sacred and their doctrines are backed by the Bible. Simply explaining that the temples are used for education, prayer, marriage, and salvation ordinances, if repeated in that manner often enough may begin to break down the stigma of the LDS faith being labeled a "secretive cult."

The Internet has provided and will continue to provide avenues and easy access for critics to attack LDS doctrine using excerpts from writings that falsely represent or paint the Church in a negative light. Often these writings are the opinions, personal journals, or public statements presumed by critics to have once been LDS doctrine. While many accuse Mormons of being ignorant of their own past, naïve, or blind to the truth of a once-sinister or deceptive past, the Bible provides commentary that reaffirms that a greater work would be performed after Christ and that God's children are accountable to the teachings of prophets and apostles in their respective dispensations.

In analyzing such criticisms brought against LDS theology chapter after chapter in this book, we can see that the Bible complements the doctrines and teachings of Joseph Smith and The Church of Jesus Christ of Latter-day Saints. Second only to the Catholic Church and the Vatican archives, the LDS Church has the largest and most detailed volume of its own history and therefore is vulnerable to such attacks. Differentiating history and doctrine or quotes and comments made in heated times, or just comprehending the context in which statements were made, demands an honest analysis before wild accusations can be accepted as truth. As previously stated, Christ's reference to a greater work and the other New Testament references of accepting God's servants validate both statements from Joseph Smith and Brigham Young.

*"And not for that nation only, but that also he should gather together in one the children of God that were scattered abroad."*

—John 11:52

*"O that I were an angel, and could have the wish of mine heart, that I might go forth and speak with the trump of God, with a voice to shake the earth, and cry repentance unto every people! Yea, I would declare unto every soul, as with the voice of thunder, repentance and the plan of redemption, that they should repent and come unto our God, that there might not be more sorrow upon all the face of the earth."*

—Alma 29:1–2

11

# Be One

## The Great Gathering

This book has sought to show what the world knows as "Mormonism" in the context of the historical narrative and in light of various biblical topics. A cycle of apostasy and restoration, the calling of prophets, and the providing of new scripture harkens back the ancient pattern seen throughout the entire Bible.

Perhaps a more complete understanding of the biblical single-faith system can lift the human consciousness to an enlightenment in which all possess the capability of making rational and loving decisions—decisions that make mankind more self-reliant, more giving, and less selfish and bring nations from instability to stability. The Bible and all scriptures are trying to express to man who God is, how he works, and how to recognize his hand in human affairs, and it is ultimately the blueprint to unite us all as God's people.

### From the "God Pattern" to Various Interpretations and Back Again

Many good deeds performed by prominent religious figures in Western religious history—such as Constantine, Bible scribes, Muhammad, Martin Luther, and other reformers—allowed sacred texts to persist through the centuries. Their experiences all varied and at times conflicted with one another over interpretation, practice, and doctrine. Yet for all this history, the biblically supported truths that Mormonism teaches came from a prophet of God, Joseph Smith. The combined history of many of these religious traditions and mankind's desire for peace created an environment of religious tolerance and free speech that allowed the Restoration of Christianity to come about.

The Catholic Church can be credited with preserving the Bible. Protestants opened the door for religious freedom, diversity, understanding, and tolerance. Muslim innovations contributed significantly—especially in science and math—toward Western advancement in technology. Yet with all the good accomplished by these religions, the message of unity still does not find a place in the current religious dialogue among Western faiths; instead, the message of faith in general continues in the spirit of division, with wars and rumors of war, especially with regard to radical Islam, the nation of Israel, and Israel's Christian supporters.

The importance of the Restoration of Christianity is that it brings us back to the pattern God expressed throughout the previous biblical dispensations. The teachings of the biblical prophets make up the core of all Western religious traditions. In the LDS Church, prophets and scripture again provide guidance for our day and are necessary for building the kingdom of God and spreading the gospel to all the earth before the second coming of our Lord.

## Be One

The purpose of this chapter is to express the importance of bringing people of faith to the next level of a biblical consciousness through responsible dialogue—dialogue that encourages and reinvigorates individual moral responsibility and an overall increase in faith God and the Bible, with less emphasis on division, name calling, and misunderstanding.

Prior to his betrayal and arrest, Jesus Christ expressed to his apostles in his great Intercessory Prayer (John 17: 20–24) his desire for man to be united as one:

> Neither pray I for these alone, but for them also which shall believe on me through their word; *That they all may be one*; as thou, Father, art in me, and I in thee, *that they also may be one in us*: that the world may believe that thou hast sent me. And the glory which

> thou gavest me I have given them; *that they may be one, even as we are one*: I in them, and thou in me, that they may be made perfect *in one*; and that the world may know that thou hast sent me, and hast loved them, as thou hast loved me.

Of all the words Jesus Christ spoke, among his final words in the Garden of Gethsemane, his prayer "that man may be one" seems to have fallen on deaf ears. How many different ways are there to interpret a particular book, chapter, or verse in the Bible? Apparently, there are enough interpretations to create the many different religions we see today. That does not sound like one God; that sounds like many—all created out of the same text.

> In those few words He made clear how the gospel of Jesus Christ can allow hearts to be made one. Those who would believe the truth He taught could accept the ordinances and the covenants offered by His authorized servants. Then, through obedience to those ordinances and covenants, their natures would be changed. . . . We can then live in unity, as we must to have peace in this life and to dwell with the Father and His Son in eternity. (Eyring, Be One)

**Civility Between Mormons and Mainstream Christians**

Elder Jeffrey R. Holland said in an address to a group of national Christian leaders, "Surely there is a way for people of goodwill who love God and have taken upon themselves the name of Christ to stand together for the cause of Christ and against the forces of sin" (Holland, *Standing Together for the Cause of Christ*). In this we have every right to be bold and believing, for "if God be for us, who can be against us?" (Romans 8:31).

Evangelical scholars Carl Moser (masters in theology, New Testament, and philosophy of religion and ethics) and Paul Owen (of the University of Edinburgh) were quoted in the *Trinity Journal* (Fall '98, 179–205) saying: "Some may criticize us for giving the Mormons too much credit and for being too harsh on our fellow evangelicals. However, much like testifying against a loved one in court, we cannot hide the facts of the matter. In this battle the Mormons are fighting valiantly." (Moser, *Mormon Scholarship, Apologetics, and Evangelical Neglect*).

Hopefully many more religious scholars and Christians alike can step forward and try to heal the plague of Christian division.

Latter-day Saints and Christianity as a whole also share important common grounds on defending religious freedoms. In fact, Chicago's Catholic archbishop, Cardinal George, spoke to students and faculty at Brigham Young University and said "that after 180 years of living mostly apart from one another, Catholics and Latter-day Saints have begun to see one another as trustworthy partners in the defense of shared moral principles" (George, *Catholics and Latter-day Saints: Partners in the Defense of Religious Freedom*).

Both churches take a common stand against pornography, gay marriage, and abortion. Many people see such stances and views in our day as bigotry, when in fact they are the opposite. God values life. Satan does not. God has laws regarding sexuality. Satan promotes promiscuity. God values and ordains marriage. Satan seeks to redefine and destroy it.

Civility and understanding must continue between faiths and are prerequisite for engaging in intelligent religious discussion that can heal our divisions. Mitchell Landsberg of the *LA Times* comments that the divisions "may reflect a reluctance by many people to dig deeply into their own beliefs and especially into those of others." In Landsberg's article, he quoted Methodist Reverend Adam Hamilton from Leawood, Kansas, saying, "I think that what happens for many Christians is, they accept their particular faith, they accept it to be true and they stop examining it. Consequently, because it's already accepted to be true, they don't examine other people's faiths. That, I think, is not healthy for a person of any faith" (Landsberg, *What do Mormons have to Offer?*). In a world of fast information, performing a quick Internet search on Mormonism will not do justice to an intelligent conversation. Many of the red flags and stigmas found in this book are perpetuated throughout the Internet. If one is seeking negative or degrading material, there should be no trouble finding it. Many go out of their way to post LDS quotes and provide their own slanderous commentary, which leads to the further stigmas. Richard J. Mouw, president and professor of Christian philosophy at Fuller Theological Seminary, recently stated, "As an Evangelical I must confess that I am ashamed of our record in relating to the Mormon community. . . . By bearing false witness against our LDS neighbors, we Evangelicals have often sinned not just against Mormons but against the God who calls us to be truth-tellers" (Mouw, *New Mormon Challenge: Responding to the Latest Defenses of Fast-Growing Movement).*

## Finding Christ's Wish of "Oneness" (John 17)

What a contradictory dilemma Christianity and the seed of Abraham face: God the Father and his Son wish for their followers to be one, yet division remains with no unity in sight. Again, there is a sense in America that rising generations are disassociating themselves more and more from traditional religious practices. Why? Perhaps because it is easy to see religion as divided when it is supposed to be based on a God who has the power to unite. This disassociation seems to fuel the fire of atheism and irreligion.

Going back through history, the Protestant Reformation opened the door of discovery for man to find the long-forgotten truths held back from the common people in centuries prior. As the Bible became more and more available, leading to the Reformation and the eventual Great Awakenings, the goal of unity was lost as division arose from of the various doctrinal interpretations that formed among many of these zealous truth-seekers. Speaking of unity, recall Paul's admonition to the Corinthians "that ye shall speak the same thing, that there be no divisions among you; but that ye be perfectly joined together" (1 Corinthians 1:10). Christians must recognize that divisions do not promote Christ's teachings and only lead to conflicts among men. These two acknowledgments are essential if we expect Christianity and Judeo-Christian values to persist and strengthen amidst the rising secular influences.

Nothing expresses what "being one with Christ" looks like in regard to obedience and building one's better self quite like Paul's words in Galatians 5:19–26. Paul contrasts the difference in the works of the flesh with the fruit of the Spirit, actions that can be taken by all mankind. Paul tells us that the "works of the flesh," which include "wrath and strife," will keep us from "inherit[ing] the kingdom of God." Paul's illustration of the fruit of the spirit express unity through our *human behavior*:

> But the fruit of the Spirit is love, joy, peace, longsuffering,

> gentleness, goodness, faith, meekness, temperance: against such there is no law. And they that are Christ's have crucified the flesh with the affections and lusts. If we live in the Spirit, let us also walk in the Spirit. Let us not be desirous of vain glory, provoking one another, envying one another. (Galatians 5:19–26)

However, reaching an agreement on all the details of history or on doctrinal issues may be less important at this moment than the agreement that Christ indeed provided the means to change human behavior. Rather than being overwhelmed by the doctrinal differences of the major religious organizations, we should focus on individual unity, beginning with one's own yearning for and application of the "fruit of the spirit" rather than the "works of the flesh." Such a fundamental change in human behavior can only allow better conditions in which the Spirit can more easily promote harmony among believers and allow for a more civil and intelligent religious discussion.

Such harmony in this case means men and women learning and applying the responsibilities of the Christian character (fruit of the spirit), while rejecting worldly trends (works of the flesh). The more that unity catches on, the less influence the world has and the more influence religious values will carry. Such an existence is the wish of Christ himself.

It is no easy task to exercise the abstinence one reads of in the Bible when a less-than-moral culture dominates the airwaves, TV, media, and academia. What information we take in on a daily basis, whether it be good or bad, can become who we are and what we do. It seems hopeless to live outside the worldly standards as Jesus commanded. In a less-than-moral world, when people stand for Christ they are increasingly mocked and pressured to do whatever it takes to feel accepted. It should be no laughing matter to strive to live the lifestyle God has commanded. If more and more people stand and defend their values, building their character to a level Jesus commanded when he admonished us to "be ye therefore perfect, even as your Father which is in Heaven is perfect" (Matthew 5:48), we can begin to see a path filled with more hope and fewer stumbling blocks.

For some, religion can often come across with the "hellfire and brimstone" approach. I believe a more Christlike approach could replace such an overwhelming approach, and compassion coupled with a thorough scriptural education will provide hope and a loving solution for those searching for truth and peace. As a disciple, simply acting as an example can provide the necessary medium for the Spirit to testify of truth and to help individuals emulate Christ. Condemning one another for our imperfections only furthers anger, division, and personal apostasy.

If Christianity continues to fail in its unifying role, mankind will continue to pursue other programs or organizations to heal society's ills, which may not necessarily involve Christ or the values that embody the Christian character.

### Unity Begins with You

The Church is a community of fellowship. Its individual members work to better their relationship with God, follow his commandments, correct their individual weaknesses, study daily on their own, and bend down quietly in prayer. Serving and loving one another leads to unity as individuals become more Christlike. Christ encouraged others to individually help the poor, the hungry, the naked, and the homeless. He taught in the Gospel of Matthew the second great commandment, "Thou shalt love thy neighbor as thyself" (Matthew 22:39). If more disciples are prepared and ready to give, and if everyone works in their own sphere of responsibility, fewer circumstances arise where people are in a panic or are left without.

Further, Elder D. Todd Christofferson, a living apostle in the LDS Church, described how the world fails to apply the teachings of God in their own lives:

> God uses scripture to unmask erroneous thinking, false traditions, and sin with its devastating effects. . . . In a complete reversal from a century ago, many today . . . argue that it's all relative or that God's love is permissive. . . . They have imagined a Jesus who wants people to work for social justice but who makes no demands upon their personal life and behavior. . . . The scriptures are the touchstone for measuring correctness and truth, and they are clear that real happiness lies not in denying the justice of God or trying to circumvent the consequences of sin but in repentance and forgiveness through the atoning grace of the Son of God. (Christofferson, *The Blessing of Scripture*)

Elder Christofferson is not suggesting that the hungry, homeless, or neglected be ignored. He seems to suggest that social justice would more positively be promoted through individual charity, righteous living, and an understanding of God's word.

To "be one" is something that can be achieved through individuals working toward the same goals. When individuals of a collective do not apply moral principles in their own lives, how can they be unified?

Cultivating Christian character can help cure most societal ills driven by impatience, greed, lying, wrath, and strife. Suffering because of occurrences beyond our control like death, natural disasters, and economic crises can be alleviated through individual responsibility, compassion, and charity. To "be one" is not only a command for an individual to take upon themselves the name of Christ; shaping one's will to that of God's has benefits that can bless the individual now, in this life, through serving his fellow man and creating an environment of safety and peace.

**Timeout: Unity**

How can one live up to "unity," and how can one express it? Here are some ideas:

- Live your life as if building God's kingdom depended on it
- Be anxiously engaged in good causes
- Free yourself from selfish addictions by coming to know Jesus Christ and learning of his Atonement; regard sex as sacred; avoid drunkenness or any substance abuse
- Serve your community in local, state, or national political offices so that issues important to you and your religious values are given a voice
- Support liberty
- Serve one another, the hungry, down-trodden, naked, and elderly
- Feast on the scriptures, fast, and pray without ceasing
- Learn God's will and prioritize your life to fulfill his will
- Be charitable toward others, both financially and socially

### Final Thoughts

Christ would not have left us without the means to be one. He meant what he said. He constantly showed others the way for the world to accomplish this and reminded us, "As I have loved you, that you also love one another" (John 13:34). We know he was the God he claimed to be, the God of the Old Testament, who called prophets and set forth his pattern and his law.

C. S. Lewis echoed Christ's sentiments when he said, "Enemy-occupied territory—that is what this world is. Christianity is the story of how the rightful king has landed, you might say landed in disguise, and is calling us all to take part in a great campaign of sabotage" (Lewis, 46). The great campaign of sabotage, of course, means sabotaging the tactics that Lucifer uses to divide us and keep us from becoming one as Christ's children. As we overcome our own lustful desires, greed, envy, hatred, dishonesty, and slothfulness, we turn our worst potential as humans into positives. If we seek to be more grateful, loving, honest, giving, and responsible in all the environments, circumstances, and every-day situations we find ourselves in, then we have "overcome the world" and have become a true disciple of Christ.

Lewis's comments resonate with Paul's words to the Romans to "be not conformed to this world: but be ye transformed by the renewing of your mind, that ye may prove what is that good, and acceptable, and perfect, will of God" (Romans 12:2). If only the world would become "one" as Christ expressed to his apostles. To take part in the "sabotage" of the world, as described by Lewis, expresses the stark distinction between Christ and the way many of us live as individuals in the world and in religious sects. A great change is needed in our hearts and minds as well as in our biblical understanding if man is to be one!

From much of this book, one might be wondering if civility can bring people of various religious backgrounds to work toward understanding and fulfilling Christ's wish. Some strides have been made among some Evangelical, Catholic, and LDS individuals as they have united to combat many social evils that threaten all religious institutions. Hopefully, the thoughts expressed in this book can create talking points and positive discussion to unite rather than divide honest seekers of truth.

"ONWARD THEN, YE PEOPLE,
JOIN OUR HAPPY THRONG.
BLEND WITH OURS YOUR VOICES
IN THE TRIUMPH SONG."

—*Onward Christian Soldiers*

# Appendices

# APPENDIX I

## ADAM, THE GOD PATTERN, AND WORLD RELIGIONS

The world's many religious traditions, Eastern (Buddhism, Taoism, Hinduism, and so on) and Western (Christianity, Islam, and Judaism), believe in and or practice a variation of the following: spirits, an afterlife, resurrection, prophets, a collection of holy writings, a great struggle between good and evil, rewards and punishments, dogmas, codes, pathways of righteousness, a creation story, a great flood, temple building, principles based on opposites, and cause and effect. So many things said and written throughout history, with language barriers and natural processes taking their toll on human artifacts, have resulted in such a great loss of what once was. How likely is it that many of these basic terms, principles, and "wild" ideas (such as resurrection, spirits, deities, and so on) entered into the minds of what were "prehistoric men" or mere biological creatures, and today make up what is a complex patchwork of human religion? What enlightened man from the very beginning?

To read the Bible and assume it happened in a time without gaps of spiritual darkness misses the point. The "one" faith existed in the Bible accordingly with each prophet and dispensation, while men created other religions. Such a premise concludes that one true faith and many man-made religions are part of the biblical or God Pattern. Man-made religions emerged to mimic God or to explain their perspectives on the different wonders of nature such as thunder, the sun, rain, and so forth. The "God Pattern" is to look at the Bible from a macro-view to see that a "single-faith system" existed as God dealt with man.

Keep the idea of the God-pattern in mind as you read the following:

It is treated amongst some historians that the Hebrew "Old Testament," does not emphasize the resurrection of the body, at least not until much later. When a practice or doctrine, such as resurrection, is introduced into a faith late into their text, historians refer to this as religious sharing or adoption through the mingling of peoples. The Egyptians, close neighbors of the Hebrews and once their masters, believed in resurrection and built these ideas into their pyramids. Again, historians believe the idea of resurrection entered the Hebrew faith through culture sharing—however, not from the Egyptians but from the Persians, who defeated Babylon and allowed the Jews to return to their homeland. Daniel from the Old Testament is credited by historians as the earliest in the Hebrew faith to speak on resurrection (Daniel 2:12) and was among the captive Hebrews. It is believed that during this time the Hebrews adopted the idea of resurrection from the Persians into their own faith. However, as discussed in chapter 5, we know the scriptures described this much earlier.

The phrase "as far as it is translated correctly" describes how Mormons view the sanctity of the Bible. Consider the biblical manuscripts for what they are: paper and ink susceptible to natural processes and human error. It is difficult to imagine that everything Moses recorded in the first five books of the Bible expresses everything God revealed to his prophets Adam, Noah, Abraham, and others, and that it remained, word for word, down until its translation into the King James Version. Further, it is difficult to imagine all that was written lasted in perfect order as revealed to the Old Testament prophets. For so long, mainstream Christians have believed the Bible was handed down in perfect form. If the Bible is not viewed realistically—as an ancient text that has been susceptible to human hands and natural conditions—anthropologists and historians have an open door to criticize the entire work. If held up as the final authority and a perfect book, the Bible can be viewed as evolutionary literature whose story adapted in time to meet man's apparent needs, or it could be said that the Bible conflicts with itself in that it first describes its followers as tribal people (Jews) who later adapted their message into a universal religion to survive (Christianity) (Reilly, 187, 203).

Can historians be blamed? If one takes the Bible as mainstream Christians take it, as being perfect, it then becomes subject to such a rigid analysis. It also becomes difficult to explain faith to "rational thinkers" who require proof. (Example: the Bible comes under attack for describing the earth's creation in only six days. Considering that none of us were there, perhaps it did take six days. Or maybe each day is a thousand or one hundred thousand years to God. Another example: did a whale really swallow Jonah? Maybe, but as a Bible believer, the moral of the story goes beyond that and neither rests nor falls on the reality of whether or not Jonah lived inside a whale for three days). LDS theology asks anyone investigating "Mormonism" to consider history but to not let historical conclusions be the end of your faith, especially if other essential factors are not considered, such as the God Pattern (the single-faith system).

Regardless of what attacks can come through a purely historical or rational approach to the Bible, the realities of cultural borrowing exist. Determining who had the "original" (as in the case of resurrection) is not so easy. Now, assume the ancestors of the Egyptians learned and adopted through cultural interaction the truths passed down from either Noah or Abraham, and one of those doctrines was resurrection. Below is from a talk given by LDS Apostle Neal A. Maxwell:

> We believe Adam and Eve were this planet's first humans and first Christians.
>
> "And thus the Gospel began to be preached, *from the beginning,* being declared by holy angels sent forth from the presence of God, and by his own voice, and by the gift of the Holy Ghost. And thus all things were confirmed unto Adam, by an holy ordinance" (Moses 5:58–59; emphasis added).
>
> Hence, brothers and sisters, a particular pattern of divine instruction followed, early on, just as occurred in the later Restoration. "Therefore [God] sent angels to converse with them, who caused men to behold of his glory. And they began from that time forth to call on his name; therefore God conversed with men, and made known unto them the plan of redemption" (Alma

> 12:29–30; see also Moses 5:58–59). However, this initial fulness was soon lost. Resulting fragmentation, diffusion, and distortion contributed to a wide variety of world religions—Christian and non-Christian. (Maxwell, *From the Beginning*)

Elder Maxwell further stated:

> President Joseph F. Smith observed that amid this diffusion certain laws and rites were "carried by the posterity of Adam into all lands, and continued with them, more or less pure, to the flood, and through Noah, . . . to those who succeeded him, spreading out into all nations and countries. . . . What wonder, then, that we should find relics of Christianity, so to speak, among . . . nations who know not Christ, and whose histories date back . . . beyond the flood, independent of and apart from the records of the Bible." (in *Journal of Discourses,* 15:325; see also Alma 29:8)

Earlier fulness was followed by periodic "famine[s]" of "hearing the words of the Lord" (Amos 8:11). Ancient Israel's fallings away were cited by Jehovah, including their changing ordinances, breaking covenants, and rebellion (see Isaiah 24:5; Ezekiel 2:3).

God (the source of truth) gave his people (Adam, Noah, and Abraham) a set of beliefs to guide them in their lives. Another group converted, broke away, or simply adopted parts of these beliefs and incorporated them into their own culture and according to their own understanding. If one compares what the Egyptians left behind, it is easy to see Egypt as being the more materially advanced society over the Hebrews. According to this theory, the Egyptians would receive credit of having invented the idea of resurrection. However, modern LDS revelation and scripture confirm that Adam, Noah, and Abraham indeed received this knowledge and much more (see Maxwell, *From the Beginning*, above).

# APPENDIX II

## THE OLD TESTAMENT AS THE STARTING POINT TO FIND THE GOD PATTERN

In further support of the Old Testament, it is well known that most cultures have their own version of the creation and a great flood. From simplistic reasoning alone it would seem to be that, as the descendents of Noah inevitably spread and separated across the earth, they carried with them the knowledge of a flood, God, and various religious principles that possibly influenced even Eastern religious traditions. Perhaps Noah or those at the Tower of Babel spoke Proto–Indo-European, the parent language of most of the world's languages. If one researches an image of the Proto–Indo-European language, the common language and split is awfully reminiscent to Genesis 11:7–8. It is of no great concern that religious stories of the world differ by some degrees, seeing that means of communication and record keeping were weak; in time, such truths would inevitably turn from a factual story to legend, myth, or something new entirely. These weaker parallels are among the hundreds of other, stronger facts that support the Old Testament text. Having this perspective lends the Old Testament unique credibility needed to provide a good starting point for finding the God Pattern.

# APPENDIX III

## BIBLICAL LAW AND SUPERSTITION

It seems to be the trend in academic and scientific communities to dismiss religious ideas because of superstition and inability to explain miracles.

Let us consider the nature of the Old Testament in relation to its peer cultures. While attending a course on weather and climate, the professor's presentation sidetracked to provide background of how man "created religion" in response to unexplainable nature or weather events. The old religions, pagan or tribal, left record (more often in oral tradition) of their superstitions in poems and dances. Natural phenomenon (the awe of severe weather or the reverence given to women for their power of childbirth) captured early man's imagination. At times devastation and unexplained phenomena led to the creation of the world's "gods," who sought to rain down vengeance and cursing.

Distinct from the Old Testament, such belief systems failed to explain man's existence, purpose, character building, and laws as seen in the Hebrew faith. Being what it is, the Hebrew faith emerged in world history as one with a purpose, stories of people, places, and events encompassing all of the human family. Stories such as Moses and the burning bush or God miraculously etching his law into stone appear to the contrary, but the essence of these events are distinct from other supernatural happenings. God would of course manifest himself in ways beyond natural explanation, but God revealing himself and pagans creating religions out of unexplainable phenomena are not the same. Yet secular circles still make these events and biblical details the focal point of their discussion, making these stories more and more the object of mockery while diverting truth seekers from the real message.

Admittedly, Deuteronomy 34:10–12 reaffirms this idea in that God uses miracles (supernatural) in times he sees fit, as with Christ, who used miracles to teach and whose message was that of a lifestyle of hope, faith, and charity. In Deuteronomy we read: "And there arose not a prophet since in Israel like unto Moses, whom the Lord knew face to face, In all the signs and the wonders which the Lord sent him to do in the land of Egypt to Pharaoh . . . which Moses showed in the sight of all Israel."

Clearly from this verse, the Bible admittedly expresses that God rarely works through the means of "signs and wonders" and that few prophets are or will be "like unto Moses." To try and superimpose the superstitious or outdated thinking of its peer cultures onto the biblical faith misses the point of the hope and practical application prophets received from the divine.

# Appendix IV

## Helpful References and Graphics

The graphics in this section are provided to help clarify some ideas mentioned throughout the book.

The "Timeline of the Single-Faith System" reflects a quick look at the story of the Bible from a macro point of view. As this book has described, the Bible is a story of God's faith system over time, with periods of "famine of the word" or apostasy. From the Fall of Adam to the enslavement of Israel and God restoring the faith through Moses, this timeline expresses where Latter-day Saints view their faith and place in Biblical history.

The "Plan of Salvation" graphic illustrates that the Bible charts the course of our spirits, living first as "the sons of God" in pre-mortality, being known before the foundation of the world, and inhabiting earth to experience life and to be judged according to our works. LDS belief in the three concepts of the pre-mortal life, man's potential to become like God, and there being various glories in the resurrection is often thought of as non-biblical; however, this chart provides evidence that the Bible teaches of this plan that God has rolled out for the purposes of his children.

# Timeline of the Single-Faith System of the Holy Bible

Many shall come in my name, saying I am Christ, and shall deceive many. —Matthew 24:5

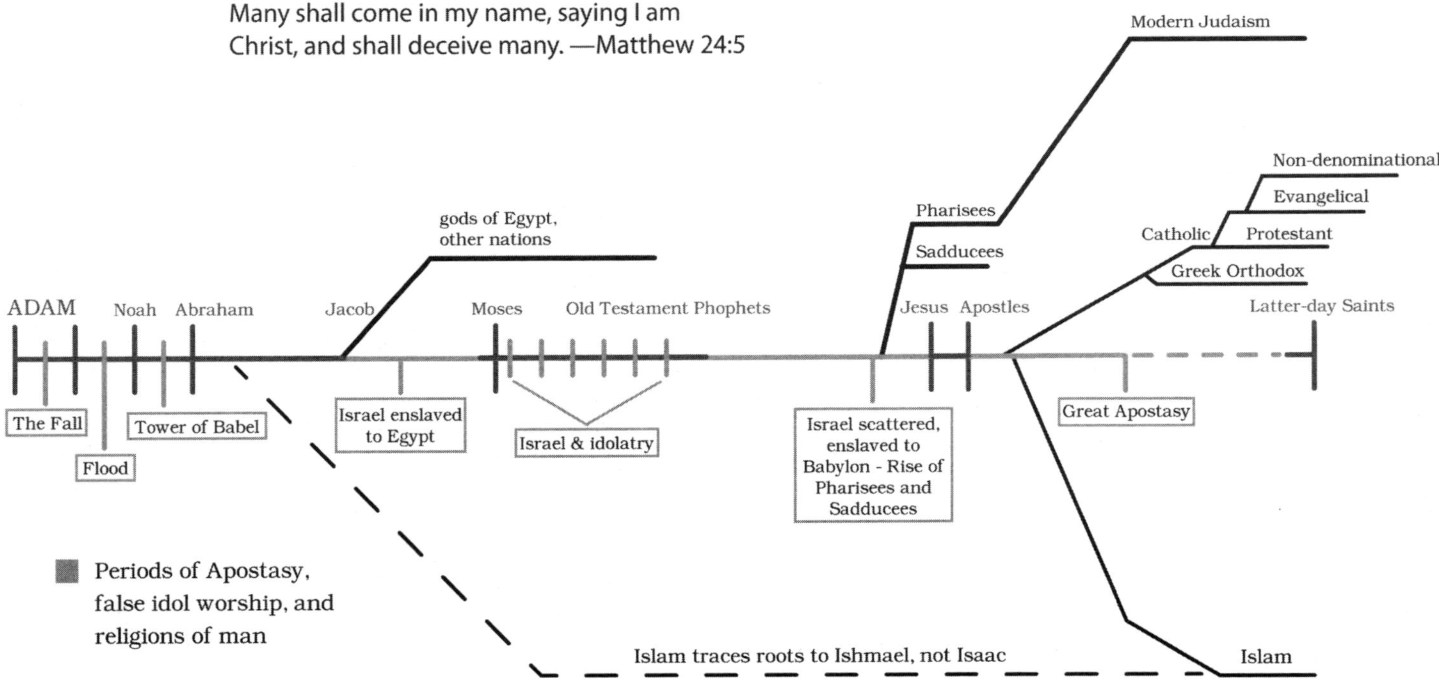


Periods of Apostasy, false idol worship, and religions of man

Periods of Restoration, called Prophets, and additional scripture

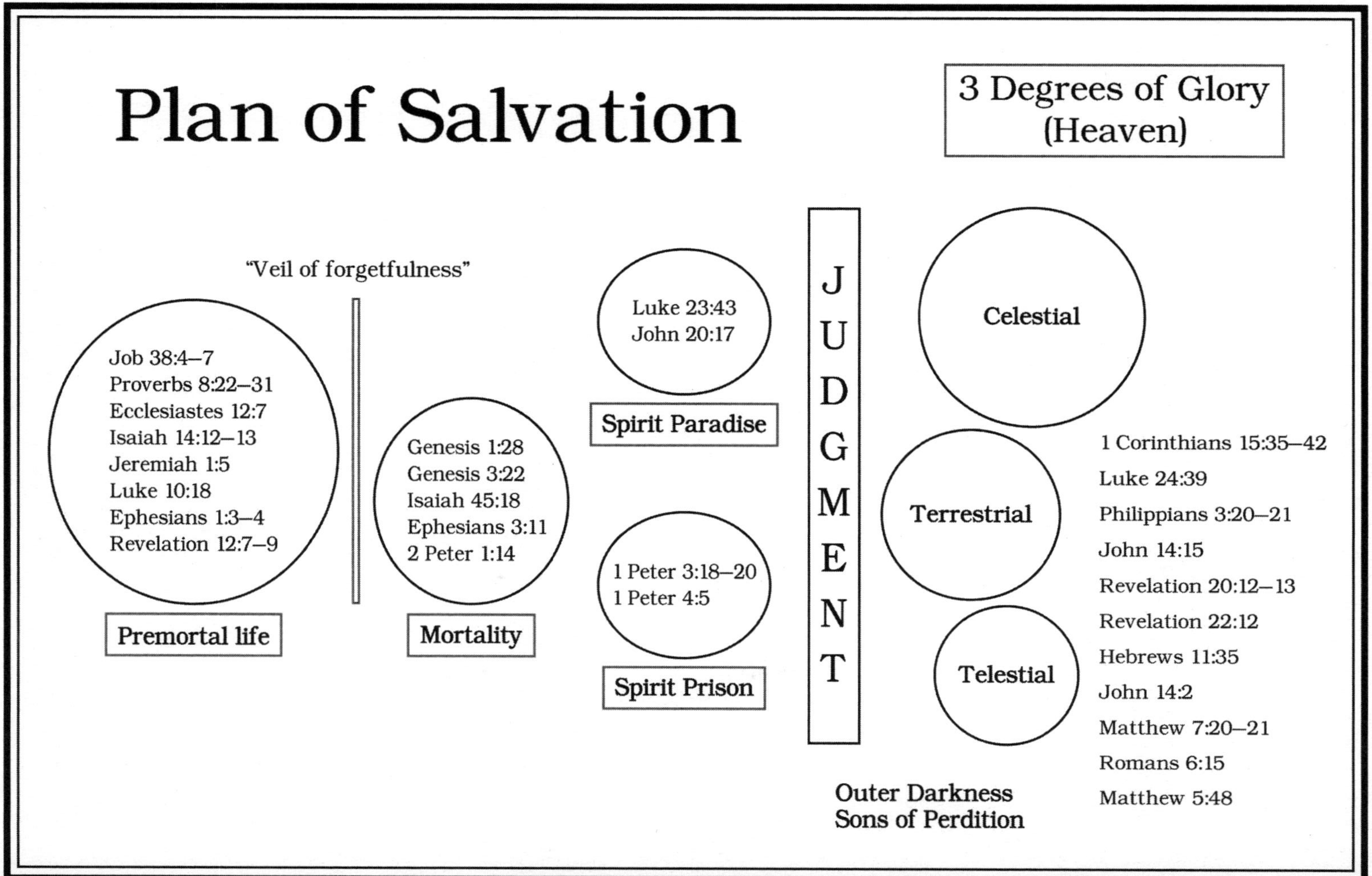

Plan of Salvation
3 Degrees of Glory (Heaven)
"Veil of forgetfulness"
Job 38:4–7
Proverbs 8:22–31
Ecclesiastes 12:7
Isaiah 14:12–13
Jeremiah 1:5
Luke 10:18
Ephesians 1:3–4
Revelation 12:7–9
Premortal life
Genesis 1:28
Genesis 3:22
Isaiah 45:18
Ephesians 3:11
2 Peter 1:14
Mortality
Luke 23:43
John 20:17
Spirit Paradise
1 Peter 3:18–20
1 Peter 4:5
Spirit Prison
JUDGMENT
Celestial
Terrestrial
Telestial
Outer Darkness
Sons of Perdition
1 Corinthians 15:35–42
Luke 24:39
Philippians 3:20–21
John 14:15
Revelation 20:12–13
Revelation 22:12
Hebrews 11:35
John 14:2
Matthew 7:20–21
Romans 6:15
Matthew 5:48

# Bibliography


Allen, C. Leonard, and Richard T. Hughes. *Discovering Our Roots: The Ancestry of Churches of Christ*. Abilene, Texas: Abilene Christian University Press, 1988.

"Americans Learned Little About the Mormon Faith, But Some Attitudes Have Softened." PEW Research, December 14, 2012. http://www.pewforum.org/Christian/Mormon/attitudes-toward-mormon-faith.aspx.

Ballard, M. Russell. "Faith, Family, Facts, and Fruits," *Ensign*, October 2007. https://www.lds.org/general-conference/2007/10/faith-family-facts-and-fruits?lang=eng.

Bickmore, Barry R. *Restoring the Ancient Church: Joseph Smith and Early Christianity*. Phoenix and Salt Lake City: Cornerstone Publishing, 1999.

Burke, Daniel. "Are Mormons Christian? It's Complicated." *The Christian Century*, January 2, 2012. http://www.christiancentury.org/article/2012-01/are-mormons-christian-its-complicated.

Bryant, William Cullen. *Picturesque America, or the Land We Live In*, volume one. New York: Appleton, 1872.

Carroll, Anne W. *Christ the King—Lord of History*, Indexed edition. Rockford, Illinois: TAN Books and Publishers, October 1994.

Christofferson, D. Todd. "The Blessing of Scripture," *Ensign*,

May 2010. http://www.lds.org/ensign/2010/05/the-blessing-of-scripture?lang=eng.

Daniel, Lillian. *Spiritual but Not Religious? Please Stop Boring Me!* United Church of Christ. August 31, 2011. http://www.ucc.org/feed-your-spirit/daily-devotional/spiritual-but-not-religious.html (Accessed March 18, 2012).

Davies, J. G. *The Early Christian Church*, New York: Anchor Books, 1965.

Eyring, Henry B. "Be One," *Ensign*, September 2008. http://www.lds.org/liahona/2008/09/be-one?lang=eng.

George, Francis. "Catholics and Latter-day Saints: Partners in the Defense of Religious Freedom." *BYU Speeches*, February 23, 2010. http://speeches.byu.edu/?act=viewitem&id=1888.

Halley, Henry H. *Halley's Bible Handbook: An Abbreviated Bible Commentary,* New Revised Edition. Grand Rapids: Zondervan Publishing, 1965.

Hatch, Edwin. *The Influence of Greek Ideas and Usage Upon the Christian Church.* London: Williams and Norgate, 1914.

Hinckley, Gordon B. *What of the Mormons? A Short History of The Church of Jesus Christ of Latter-day Saints,* Sixth Edition Revised, The Church of Jesus Christ of Latter-day Saints, 1954.

Holguin, Jaime. *Science Unlocks Biblical Secrets, David Hawkins Reports It Took Modern Technology to Prove Antiquity of Biblical Scrolls.* CBS News, March 25, 2005. http://www.cbsnews.com/stories/2005/03/25/eveningnews/main683239.shtml.

Holland, Jeffrey R. "Standing Together for the Cause of Christ," *Ensign*, August 2012. http://www.lds.org/ensign/2012/08/standing-together-for-the-cause-of-christ?lang=eng&query=christian+unity+(name%3a%22Jeffrey+R.+Holland%22).

"I Have A Question," *Ensign*, October 1978. http://www.lds.org/ensign/1978/10/i-have-a-question/i-have-a-question?lang=eng&query=%22three+gods%22.

Johnson, Franks J., and Rabbi William J. Leffler. *Jews and Mormons: Two Houses of Israel.* Hoboken, NJ: Ktav Publishing, 2000.

Landsberg, Mitchell. *Atheists, agnostics most knowledgeable about religion, survey says.* September 28, 2010. *Los Angeles Times.* http://articles.latimes.com/2010/sep/28/nation/la-na-religion-survey-20100928.

LDS FAIR, "Mormonism and the nature of God/God is a Spirit." http://en.fairmormon.org/Mormonism_and_the_nature_of_God/God_is_a_Spirit.

Leonard, Glen M. *Nauvoo, A Place of Peace, A People of Promise,* Salt Lake City: Deseret Book, 2002.

Lewis, C. S. *Mere Christianity,* New York: HarperCollins, 2001.

Lloyd, Scott R. "'Be Ready' to Defend Faith." *Church News.* August 10, 2010. http://www.ldschurchnews.com/articles/59708/Be-Ready-to-Defend-Faith.html.

Man from Modesto, "Head to Head: Mormonism vs. Christianity." http://manfrommodesto.hubpages.com/hub/Head-to-Head-Mormonism-vs-Christianity.

Martel, Frances. "To Anderson Cooper: Romney May Belong To A 'Cult,' But He Is Better Than Obama." October 8, 2011. http://www.mediaite.com/tv/anti-mormon-pastor-to-anderson-cooper-romney-may-belong-to-a-cult-but-he-is-better-than-obama.

Maxwell, Neal A. "From the Beginning," *Ensign*, November 1993. http://www.lds.org/ensign/1993/11/from-the-beginning?lang=eng.

McConkie, Bruce R. *Mormon Doctrine,* Salt Lake City: Bookcraft, 1966.

Meyers, Gary D. "'Silver scrolls' are oldest Old Testament scripture, archaeologist says," *BP News.* February 27, 2004. http://www.bpnews.net/bpnews.asp?id=17741.

"Mitt Romney finds Christian support: Still standing is not secure with evangelicals," *Associated Press*. October 24, 2007. http://www.msnbc.msn.com/id/21451031/ns/politics-decision_08/.

*Mormons in America: Certain in Their Beliefs, Uncertain of Their Place in Society*. POLL, January 12, 2012. http://www.pewforum.org/Christian/Mormon/mormons-in-america-executive-summary.aspx.

Mosser, Carl. Paul Owen. *Mormon Scholarship, Apologetics, and Evangelical Neglect: Losing the Battle and Not Knowing It?* http://www.cephasministry.com/mormon_apologetics_losing_battle.html.

Mouw, Richard J. forward to the *New Mormon Challenge: Responding to the Latest Defenses of Fast-Growing Movement*, ed. Francis J. Beckwith, Carl Mosser, and Paul Owens (Grand Rapids, Mich.: Zondervan, 2002).

*New Testament Study Guide*. Salt Lake City: The Church of Jesus Christ of Latter-day Saints, 2003. http://www.lds.org/manual/print/new-testament-student-study-guide/the-gospel-according-to-saint-john/john-2-jesus-begins-his-work?lang=eng.

Ostling, Richard N. and Joan K. *Mormon America the Power and the Promise*. New York: HarperCollins, 1999.

Peck, Garrett. *The Prohibition Hangover*. http://www.prohibitionhangover.com/israelwine.html.

Reilly, Kevin. *Worlds of History: A Comparative Reader*, volume one, third edition. Boston: Bedford/St. Martin's, 2007.

Reynolds, M. H. "The Truth About Roman Catholicism," *Christian News and Views Newsletter and Resource Page* (reprinted from *Foundation Magazine*, vol. XIII, issue 1). Los Osos, CA: Fundamental Evangelistic Association. http://cnview.com/on_line_resources/the_truth_about_roman_catholics_final.htm.

Richards, LeGrand *A Marvelous Work and A Wonder,* Salt Lake City: Deseret Book, 1976.

Stack, Peggy Fletcher. "Are Mormons primed for persecution in this election season?" *The Salt Lake Tribune*. June 9, 2012. http://www.sltrib.com/sltrib/news/54270180-78/bednar-church-clayton-faith.html.csp.

Tanner, Sandra. "Terminology Differences." http://www.utlm.org/onlineresources/terminologymain.htm.

Tertullian, *Against Praxeas*. LaVergne, TN: Kessinger Publishing, 2010. http://www.britannica.com/facts/5/176203/Sixtus-IV-as-discussed-in-inquisition-Roman-Catholicis.

Slick, Matt., "What is the New Age Movement?" *Christian Apologetics and Research Ministry* (CARM). http://carm.org/new-age-what.

Walker, Joseph. *Looking for understanding in the Mormon spotlight*. July 1, 2011. Salt Lake City: Deseret News. http://www.deseretnews.com/article/700148615/Looking-for-understanding-in-the-Mormon-spotlight.html.

Walker, Joseph. "Journalists urged to allow Mormons to define themselves." December 8, 2011. Salt Lake City: Deseret News. http://www.deseretnews.com/article/700205386/Journalists-urged-to-allow-Mormons-to-define-themselves.html.

Wilcox, Brad. "His Grace if Sufficient." July 12, 2011. http://speeches.byu.edu/?act=viewitem&id=1966.

# INDEX


A

Afterlife: *63*

Alcohol: *xviii, 102–3*

Angels: *84*

Apostasy: *xvi, 4, 11–15, 17, 86, 94, 98, 115, 121*

Apostles: *xvi, 2, 4–7, 9, 10, 12–20, 23, 26–27, 30–32, 34, 59, 78–79, 82–83, 88, 92, 94, 95–101, 104, 107, 110–12, 116, 123*

B

Ballard, M. Russell: *xviii*

Baptism for the dead: *xvii, 78, 88, 97, 108*

Bishops: *26, 70*

Book of Mormon: *xviii, 3, 34, 39, 43–44, 49, 68, 75, 81–89*

C

Catholic: *6, 20–21, 24–27, 34–35, 73, 89, 98, 107, 113, 116, 118, 123*

Celestial kingdom. **See** DEGREES OF GLORY

Christ, Jesus. **See** JESUS CHRIST

Christofferson, D. Todd: *121–22*

Cross: *25, 29, 67, 71, 75–78, 89, 106, 112*

Cult: *xiv, 8, 36–37, 44, 58, 91–92, 97, 99, 112*

D

Defend: *xviii, 120*

Degrees of glory: *66, 69–71, 73, 75, 77, 79*

## E

Easter: *97*

Evangelical: *52, 117–18, 123*

## G

Godhead: *28, 29, 30, 31, 36, 53, 97, 105*

Gods (gods): *xvii, 1, 7, 13, 29, 41, 43, 47, 52,–58, 60, 66, 82, 135*

Gold Plates: *84*

Grace: *xvii, 13, 15, 50, 53, 73–77, 79, 121*

## H

Holland, Jeffrey R.: *24, 52, 117*

Holy Ghost: *30, 52, 78–79, 95, 104, 109, 131*

## I

Idols, idolatry, graven images: 7, *13, 55, 58–59, 60*

Infant Baptism: *33*

Islam, Muslims: *xvi, xviii, 1–4, 6, 9, 11–12, 26, 57, 116, 129*

## J

Jeffress, Robert: *92, 98*

Jesus Christ: *xv, 2, 5, 8–10, 20, 28–29, 31, 35, 46, 50–51, 53–55, 67, 70, 77, 82, 85, 88, 97, 108, 110, 113, 116–117, 122*

Jews: *1–5, 9, 14, 26–27, 32, 64, 130–31*

## L

Lewis, C. S.: *xvi, xviii, 52–53, 105, 123*

Lucifer: *47–48, 50–51, 59, 123*. **See also** SATAN

## M

Martyr, Justin: *31, 96*

Maxwell, Neal A.: *131–132*

Monotheism: *29, 60*

Muhammad: *2–4, 115*

## O

Ordinances: *34, 37, 108, 109, 131*

Origen: *xviii, 31, 96*

Ostling, Richard and Joan: *43*

## P

Perry, Rick: *92*

Pharisees: *5, 7, 13–14, 23, 94*

Plural Marriage: *40, 45, 97*. **See also** POLYGAMY

Polygamy: *xiv, xv, xvii, 39, 42–43, 45*. **See also** PLURAL MARRIAGE

Polytheism: *47–48, 55, 60, 63*

Popes: *27*

Premortal life: *47–52, 59–60, 89*

Priesthood: *17–18, 94*

Prophets: *xvi, 1, 3–7, 9–14, 17–20, 23, 25–27, 30, 32, 36, 44, 56, 68, 82, 86, 88–89, 92, 94–96, 98–101, 111–112, 115–116, 123, 129–130, 136*

Protestant: *xvi–xvii, 6, 15, 26, 28, 36, 92, 98, 119*

Protestant Reformation: *6, 15, 26, 28, 98, 119*

## Q

Quorum of the Seventy: *95*

Qu'ran: *4*

## R

Restoration: *xiii, xiv, xviii, xix, 2, 12, 36, 65, 91, 93, 95, 98–99, 101, 104, 116, 131, 151*

Resurrection: *xvii, 48, 51–52, 62–69, 78–79, 82, 96–97, 107, 129–32*

Romney, Mitt: *7–8*

## S

Sadducees: *5, 13, 23, 94*

Saint (Saints): *xiv, 17, 23, 35, 37*

Satan: *34, 50, 53, 92, 118*

Smith, Joseph: *xv, xvi, xviii, 2, 7, 12–19, 21, 24, 29, 30–31, 34, 36, 42, 44, 52, 55, 57, 60, 66, 68, 81–88, 90–92, 94–98, 101–102, 108, 110–111, 113, 116*

Smith, Joseph F.: *53, 132*

T

Tanner, Sandra: *48*

Telestial. **See** DEGREES OF GLORY

Temples: *5, 14, 41, 42, 73, 78, 88, 107–108, 110, 129*

Terrestrial. **See** DEGREES OF GLORY

Tertullian: *31, 96*

Trinity: *xvi, 23–24, 28, 30–31, 36, 102, 117*

U

Unity: *xviii, 4, 8, 24, 27, 30–31, 98, 116–117, 119–122*

W

Williams, Roger: *94*

Works: *xix, 40, 49, 71–79, 88–89, 97, 102, 108, 110, 115, 119–121, 136*

Y

Young, Brigham: *42, 101, 111, 113, 118*

# About the Author

Scott Thormaehlen served honorably for four years in the United States Air Force as a weather forecaster from 2000 to 2004. In 2010 he graduated from the University of Texas at San Antonio with a BA in history. These academic and professional experiences cultivated his already analytical and curious mind.

Having lived thirty years in the "mission field," Scott gained a cultural perspective of his religious counterparts in school and among friends, neighbors, and coworkers. Sharing a belief in the Bible and being raised in the knowledge of the Restoration, Scott came to realize the peculiarity of his station in life and the conflict between Mormonism and mainstream Christians. Knowing what he was taught to be true, he felt compelled to share his experiences and lessons of his faith and bring them the LDS audience. His interest in history—particularly early Christian history and the differences between Mormons and mainstream Christians—motivated this book. The first few pages of this book were written in 2003 as notes meant to simply answer questions about Mormon topics with responses from the Bible. Over the years, Scott added more notes until he decided to divide them topically, do more research, and put his work into book format.

Scott is a direct descendant of Mormon pioneer Levi Savage, whose descendants settled in Samaria and Malad in Southern Idaho and is the great-grandson of Samaria's Gillespie Waldron, famous for his tales of buried treasure, an iron door, and a shootout among gold thieves. Scott also has Texas gunfighter heritage on his dad's side. He loves his family, the outdoors, reading nonfiction, and politics. Scott currently resides in Provo, Utah, and is the marketing and events coordinator at Cedar Fort, Inc.

0 26575 11725 7